# LIFT

## The Joy of a Life in Flight

## Wally Obermeyer

*with Helen Obermeyer*

LIFT PRESS

LIFT PRESS



Paperback ISBN: 979-8994516911
Ebook ISBN: 979-8994516904


Laura Zigman, Co-writer and Editorial Collaborator
Laura Obermeyer, Photo Researcher
Catherine Ward, Researcher

Book production by The Pub Pros, Inc., www.thepubpros.com
Dan Avant Blachman, Copyeditor
Elizabeth Blachman, Proofreader
Maria Gagliano, Project Director
Celia Blue Johnson, Developmental Editor
Karl Spurzem, Cover and Interior Designer

*To the women in my life who put ego aside and get the work done.
You have helped me be the very best version of myself.
I am filled with gratitude.*

*Natalie, Kyra, and Catherine, who have made me whole.*

*Ali, Dana, and Chris, who helped me realize my professional
aspirations and through it all have become my dear friends.*

*Nome, who helped me believe in myself and gave me the gift
of knowledge.*

*Helen, you are my everything. I am waiting.*

# CONTENTS

lift

/'lift/

*Verb:*
to raise from a lower to a higher position: elevate

*Noun:*
an elevating influence

an elevation of the spirit

an apparatus or machine used for hoisting,
such as a ski lift

the amount that may be lifted at one time: load

the component of the total aerodynamic force acting on
an airplane or airfoil that is perpendicular to the relative
wind and that for an airplane constitutes the upward
force that opposes the pull of gravity

*—Merriam-Webster Dictionary*

# INTRODUCTION

Every December, my wife, Helen, puts together a photo album to collect the highlights of the past year, and when she does, she always asks for my phone so that she can add my pictures to the ones she has on hers. By now, after almost twenty years together, she knows what she'll find on my camera roll: clouds; airstrips; aerial views of mountains and rivers, deserts and plains; more clouds; the sun sparkling off the silver tip of a wing in the air; my plane on the ground at the airport or parked in the hangar. Flying is pure joy for me, and my passion for it approximates romantic love. No wonder she rightly refers to the planes I've owned and flown as "the other women." I remember each one the way I remember meaningful relationships—where we met and the experiences we shared—as well as actual plane-related things too, like the beauty of their paint jobs and the specifics of their tail numbers and upgrades. What I tell almost everyone when I first meet them is not where I went to school or where I'm from but how much I love flying: being aloft and unfettered by gravity, feeling both completely focused and completely free at the same time. I think it's the thing that defines me most.

There are many metaphors about flying that are relevant to life, but the most important one to me is the all-encompassing sense of lift: the act of elevating the spirit, of creating joy for yourself and others, of giving those you care about a special and memorable experience.

My motivation for writing this book was never to produce a memoir. I wanted instead to show how the experiences I was lucky enough to have as a child and young adult in Aspen in the 1960s, '70s, and '80s helped me develop a set of principles that informed most of the decisions I've made throughout my personal life and in starting and building Obermeyer Wealth Partners (OWP). The lessons I learned from the family that raised me and the time and place I grew up in shaped every aspect of who I am and what is of fundamental importance to me: to care deeply, to love fully, to follow my own path, and to find joy and fun and connection in everything I do.

Relationships last when people feel cared for. In the same way, an investment advisory business lasts because people know when they're understood, when their needs are met, and when they believe that those they've entrusted with their life savings are there to serve them and will always do the honorable thing. They can feel it. The values that I carried from childhood to OWP are somewhat unique in the industry now, quaint even, but they're at the core of everything we do. Every conversation we have with a client, every decision we make on their behalf, every question we ask is designed to help us more fully understand who each person is: where they came from, how they were raised, what their lives and dreams look like. I'm so grateful to have found such an incredible team to grow the business with, a team who shares these values, and I'm honored to serve clients who share these values too. I feel lucky every day to do what I do.

Warren Buffett has said and written many things that resonate deeply with me, and one of them is this: "A rising tide floats all boats; only when the tide goes out do you discover who's been swimming naked." Since studying economics in college, I've believed that the capitalist system, when combined with an abiding ethical base and in service of the betterment of society at large, is the best system in the world for benefiting the majority of people. No philosophy, religion, or institutional belief system is perfect—we all know that when they're exploited in the service of individual power and greed, they become a destructive force—but at its core, the free market flow of capital in service of private growth of business and production of services gives us the best chance of raising the standard of living and lifting us all up together.

Over the past three decades that I've spent building a registered investment advisory business, I've come to realize that there is no one right way to help people grow and maintain their wealth, their lifetime of stored labor—it's as much an art as a science to balance risk and reward. The outcomes are always uncertain, there are no guarantees, and for most of us, taking a series of limited and calculated bets works best in the long run. Much-needed calm can come from understanding and accepting the fact that investing is historically cyclical: What goes down will, eventually, recover and come back up.

I've also learned that some of the most important questions I can ask someone relate to how they think about money and how they define wealth and success: *What does money actually mean to you? When will you feel you have enough? What is the difference for you between money and wealth?* Everyone has different answers to these questions, because we're all wired differently, and we all have different goals and priorities. Over the years, I've found that most people are the happiest and feel the most secure—the most wealthy—when they focus on helping others. In the end, it may be that our connections to friends, family, colleagues, and neighbors are what matter most. That's what matters most to me. The greatest privilege of my career has been the relationships I've built with the clients I've served and learned from, and with the extraordinary people who form our team at OWP.

So, how do I define wealth? It's listening to one of my colleagues in the office lunchroom tell me about the new house they bought, or the baby they just brought into the world, and knowing I've built a business that has allowed people to feel stable enough to take on those responsibilities. Wealth is holding my daughter Natalie's first child for the first time; spending a day skiing or hiking with my family and coming back to a warm and comfortable home full of memories from the decades I've lived there; watching everyone pitch in to cook a delicious dinner, then curling up on the couch with my daughters and knowing that I've played a small part in helping them feel secure and happy when they share stories of their lives with me. Wealth is enjoying a cold beer and some salami and cheese with the best of friends at a mountain hut in the Alps; digging my toes into the sand at the beach, coffee cup in hand, while watching the sky turn pink before anyone else has woken up; waiting for the last of my family to arrive at the summit of Kilimanjaro just as the sun rises over the horizon. Wealth is seeing the happiness on the faces of my in-laws when we present them with a new puppy; sitting with my dad and Nome as the deer arrive to eat a few apples and settle in for the night; standing at the window in a moment of deepest despair and having my wife walk in and wrap me in her arms and say "I know" without my having to utter a word; looking at photos on my phone and remembering all the times we've been in the air together, unfettered by gravity, lifted by joy.

These are the moments when I know that I'm the wealthiest, and happiest, man alive.

takeoff
/ˈtāk-ˌȯf/

*Noun:*
a rise or leap from a surface in making a jump or flight
or an ascent in an aircraft or in the launching of a rocket

an action of starting out

a rapid rise in activity, growth, or popularity

a spot at which one takes off

a starting point: point of departure

*—Merriam-Webster Dictionary*

# BUMPY START

In all my years of helping people create lives of wealth and stability, I've learned that everyone has a story, and most of those stories include hard work, determination, overcoming adversity, and perseverance. Mine certainly does. Growing up in storied Aspen, Colorado, in a locally famous ski-legend family sounds like a fairy tale or a movie, given all the usual assumptions about privilege being a guaranteed entry into a life of happiness and ease, but those are only partial truths. The full landscape of my childhood was a bit more complicated than that.

I was born on Halloween in 1956 to Esther Obermeyer (née Comrie) and Klaus F. Obermeyer. Klaus and Esther met in Sun Valley, Idaho. Klaus was fleeing a past in Germany and pursuing his passion for skiing. He came to America from Germany in 1947, a story I will go into later in this book. My mother, who went by the name EJ, was a beauty and a great athlete from the Midwest with an adventurous spirit and an equal love of skiing. She was an ice skater in the famous *Sun Valley on Ice* show at the Sun Valley Lodge when Klaus arrived in Idaho. He had set out with a promise from Friedl Pfeifer, a renowned skier from Austria whom Klaus had known from his early days in Germany, that he could teach skiing, only to find that Friedl had left for Aspen. So Klaus took on odd jobs to make enough money to get to Aspen, including repping ski equipment with Warren Miller (who went on to become famous for his extreme skiing movies). Klaus and EJ met in town; shortly after they were married, they moved to Aspen, and Klaus finally caught up with Friedl and commenced teaching skiing. Klaus built them a Bavarian-style chalet near the base of Buttermilk Mountain, where most people who come to the four ski areas known collectively as Aspen start learning to ski. I imagine they had a lot of fun together on the slopes and with the exciting clients who returned every year to learn from Klaus and bask in his magnetic personality and indomitable passion for the sport—prominent business types and intellectuals involved in the early years of the Aspen Institute, like Walter Paepcke, Herbert Bayer, and Mortimer Adler; and the Hollywood set that included Gary Cooper, Ethel Merman, Hedy Lamarr, Lana Turner, and Ray Milland.

After a year or so they decided to start a family. My brother, Henry Carl Obermeyer, was born in April 1954, I followed two and a half years later, and baby Susan came five years after me.

Klaus quickly realized that his biggest challenge was keeping his clients warm and dry on the slopes long enough for them to learn to link turns and have fun getting from the 11,212-foot summit of Aspen Mountain to the ski lodges and bars at its 8,000-foot base. He started importing skiwear from Germany, Austria, and Switzerland and turned it into a business that eventually eclipsed giving skiing lessons as his primary source of income. Sport Obermeyer continues to be driven by the mission to keep people comfortable in the harshest of conditions.

For us kids, Aspen was our playground. In the summer, sheep grazed the slopes, keeping them free of trees and bushes, readying the terrain for nice clean runs after the next snowfall. The clear blue Colorado skies and sunshine made famous in John Denver's ballads were my reality. It was a small town in those days, Highway 82 still a two-lane dirt road, and our family knew almost everyone who lived in the valley. I could walk into Matthew Drug, now Carl's Pharmacy, sit up at the bar, and order my favorite black-and-white milkshake knowing that the bill would somehow get paid. The residents were there for the mountain life—healthy living and a relaxed sense of time that revolved around Mother Nature's schedule. The long days of summer were filled with projects, picnics, fishing, camping; the cold, short days of winter with skiing, skating, fires, early nights, and long breakfasts. This idyllic-sounding childhood gave me a passion for everything that mountain living had to offer: fishing, hunting, hiking, horseback riding. Our days were spent almost wholly outdoors, exploring endless expanses unsupervised. I couldn't have been born into luckier circumstances.

Unbeknownst to me as a young child, though, were the strains on my parents' marriage, which was unraveling. It was the 1960s, there were "distractions," and while the family narrative about exactly what happened between them remains unclear, the upshot was that they separated, and their separation had a tremendous effect on my mother's mental health. Today we understand a lot more about the biology of postpartum depression, but back then it was just mental illness. Whether her depression caused their split or the split caused her illness I will never know, but what I do know is that my mom fell apart during that time, and when she did, we children were totally neglected. Despite how hard she tried to keep it together alone with the three of us after my father moved out, Henry and I often went days without being fed. Books were prohibited in the house, we were not read to, and we were not looked after. Neighbors were aware of our situation and helped where and how they could, but Colorado is the West, and neighbors tend to stay out of each other's business.

During this time, while we were still living in the chalet my parents had shared on what is now the grounds of the Maroon Creek Club across from the Buttermilk ski area, Dad was constantly busy growing his skiwear company. He bought a warehouse and a miners' cabin in downtown Aspen, which became his primary focus and gave us even more unsupervised time outdoors. We would put on our skis and walk across Highway 82, trying not to pick up too much dirt from the road in the wax on the bottom of our skis, and take the T-bar up to the top of the mountain, making endless laps up and down the slopes for days on end. In summer, after chores, we hiked, biked, and fished.

Henry has always been a gifted and creative builder of things, and we spent hours improving our bicycles and making catapults, forts, bridges, and better skis—everything for our outdoor life. He loved going to the dump and finding things that might be useful in some way, like a part for building an electric eye, which he hooked up to a little cannon in our room to shoot rubber bullets at anyone who entered uninvited. In later years, he won the high school science fair for developing a seismograph that was more sensitive than anything the government had developed. And when the military got wind of his invention, they sent a helicopter to fly him down to White Sands, New Mexico, for a debriefing. As a junior in high school, he was recruited to enter the prestigious Colorado School of Mines as a very young freshman, which confirmed what we'd always known: that he was truly an engineering genius. It also confirmed that he'd clearly been fibbing about the laundry machines being too challenging for him and was just adding to his younger brother's pile of chores. Susan was not there to help me either, as by this time the courts had decided she was too young to be separated from my mother.

Though he was my best friend and confidant, and as close as we were as brothers, Henry could at times retreat into his interior life and ignore what was going on at home, hiding in his room or disappearing into whatever part of the house he was making his next creation in, leaving me to feel even more alone. Luckily, I was often taken in by our next-door neighbor Mrs. Mayer, who loved to make me sandwiches and treats and frequently invited me over for dinner. At seven years old, I was as hungry for that kind of care and attention as I was for food, and I knew, even then, that I would need to course-correct and find a way through and past our bumpy start in life.

# SAVED BY NOME

Right as I realized that spending as much time as possible out of our mother's house would be crucial to my survival, my dad met a strikingly attractive woman at the Hotel Jerome, where he often ate breakfast and she was waitressing. Nome (née Margaret Hepburn Perry) had left the East Coast in the early 1960s to go to New Mexico to give birth to a baby whose father had disappeared. Nome knew that she was too young to take on the responsibility of raising a child by herself and decided to put the baby up for adoption. After the baby was born and not eager to return to judgmental New England gossips, she started driving; when she stopped in Aspen, she stayed. Nome had the same fierce determination and wild spirit as her aunt Katharine Hepburn. Nome and Klaus spent more and more time together, and they married in June 1965. She was twenty-two and he was forty-four, but age never seemed to matter to her, then or now.

Once Nome came into our family, she saw what was going on with her husband's children and knew she had to get involved. She had her own sadness around the loss of her child who had been adopted, and focusing on us was her way of filling and healing that heartache. The arrival of Nome for me started what would become one of the biggest gifts of my life. I took one look at her and she at me, and the trajectory of our futures changed for the better. Wanting to spend as much time as I could with Dad and Nome, I started running away from my mother's house regularly—before I was even ten, I remember crossing the Roaring Fork River after spring thaw to walk to the miners' cabin that they had converted into a home right next to the warehouse, in the middle of downtown Aspen at the location that is now the Obermeyer Place office and condominium complex.

I like to say that at that tender age I adopted Nome and she adopted me. Nome was warmth and love and salami sandwiches slathered in mayonnaise and homemade cookies and books and stories and everything a physically and emotionally starving nine-year-old boy could want. I was a sponge for her teaching and her outlook on life. She taught me what being taken care of felt like, and in that way, and many others, she saved me—who knows what would have become of me had she not? But a child doesn't have the authority or knowledge to navigate the legal system around divorce and custody: All I knew was that I had to try and spend as much time with Dad and Nome as I could. And to do that, I had to be a good boy. I had to figure out what the parents needed, and do it. My constant running away eventually got the attention of the local police and would eventually spark one of the most contentious custody lawsuits in Colorado.

My first memory of a run-in with the law around this issue was in the Pitkin County Courthouse: Henry and I were present for a proceeding, and when EJ's lawyer tried to grab both of us to leave, Dad's lawyer, a wonderful man named Leslie Gross, would not allow it. "Get your hands off those boys until this case is decided," he boomed. The judge agreed, and we soon started splitting time between EJ's and Dad's, spending most of the summer with Dad.

One of the first summers while custody was still being figured out, Henry and I went to the family farm where Nome had grown up in northwest Connecticut. Her family was as fierce about protecting Henry and me as she was, and her mother, Mrs. Perry, took us in like her own children, giving us lessons in New England etiquette and manners. Every night Mr. Perry directed our attention to the blackboard that was a permanent fixture in the dining room, where history, literature, and engineering lessons were discussed. We went to the shore and stayed at Katharine Hepburn's—"Aunt Kat's"—home in Old Saybrook on Long Island Sound, where we learned to swim with her in the frigid Atlantic, ate clams and mussels, cursed, and heard stories of her days drinking gin with Humphrey Bogart and John Huston on the set of *The African Queen*. Aunt Kat even took me to the Brown Palace Hotel in Denver on my fourteenth birthday and ordered me my first drink.

"Bring the boy a whiskey," she said, and they did. No waiter was going to ask her if I was of age.

But it wasn't long before the FBI showed up to investigate whether Henry and I had, as EJ's lawyer alleged, been kidnapped. We hid in the closet while Mrs. Perry gave the agents a piece of her mind and watched as they left with their tails between their legs. Another time, when I was ten and Henry was twelve and the raging lawsuit over custody was still in full swing, we were told that we'd have to go to EJ's parents' house in Grand Rapids, Michigan, for half the summer. Whatever the parents and lawyers were up to was irrelevant to Henry and me—we had no intention of staying in the home of grandparents we barely knew. Adding insult to injury, we found out that EJ had rented another house for herself and Susan because our younger sister "was too happy to see us," so we weren't even going to be able to play with her. Henry and I realized then that EJ had gone over the edge. We had no desire to go there with her.

Henry and I were young and angry and caught in the middle of a never-ending legal battle that seemed to have no interest in considering what we wanted, which was simply to get out of Michigan and live permanently with our father and Nome back in Colorado. One night, very late, we hatched another plan to run away: We wrote notes in crayon on the walls of the room we were staying in, grabbed as much food as we could find in the pantry, snuck out the window, and took off. For two days, we lived along the railroad tracks like hobos, not sure what our actual plan was but knowing it would have something to do with hopping a train west. When we found what seemed to be an already-constructed shelter made of scrap wood and tarp and tried to sleep in it, we were chased out by a very hairy and scary character with a big bowie knife, an experience that may have softened us a bit on the romance of the wandering life.

Our adventure was cut short when the police eventually found us. There was no obvious place for us to go that night, since EJ and her parents and Nome and Klaus were all claiming custody, so, like all common criminals, we ended up in the local jail. It was grim and stark and not at all what we had in mind for the rest of our lives, and in our exhaustion, as we discussed our plight and our diminishing options, Henry said out loud that he wished they would turn off the lights so he could sleep. When his wish came true and darkness fell immediately, we knew they'd listened to our entire conversation and had probably even recorded it. In time, likely because of the very obvious lack of EJ's parenting ability and our fierce determination to stay with Dad and our strong and dedicated stepparent Nome, the Colorado courts did something they had never done before: They granted Klaus full custody of Henry and me and gave EJ full custody of baby Susan.

The decision was a win for us two, but it was also a sad loss for us three siblings: We would be separated from our little sister for a long while. With the custody battle finally over and the dust settling, a whole new chapter in my life was about to begin, and I couldn't wait for a fresh start and a more stable homelife.

# HOME ALONE

Life settled into a very different routine with Nome as our official new mother. She had grown up on a big working farm in Connecticut—120 acres where they grew their own food, butchered their own meat, and made their own bread. They had lived in an 1840s stone house that, in their early years there, didn't have running water, central heating, or electricity—and she was determined to recreate the same environment for herself and for us in the West. She and Dad bought 150 acres in Emma, Colorado, along the Roaring Fork River, land that had been owned by Italian fruit growers—over the years, apricots, plums, pears, and six different kinds of apples that intentionally matured at different times had been planted, so there were always perfectly ripe fruits all summer and fall. Then came the exciting arrival in 1968 of my new baby brother, Klaus Junior, also known as Klausie or Peeky. All the love Nome had bestowed on Henry and me was exponentially redirected to this towheaded, energetic, adorable child we all spoiled to death. Klausie could do no wrong; he became the sun around which our parents' days revolved. Once again, life shifted.

By the time we moved to Emma, Henry and I were considered old enough to be farmhands. We were taught how to dig postholes and fence pastures and how to care for and slaughter sheep and pigs, goats and rabbits. We learned the seasonality of flood irrigation and haying. We got strong and healthy. Later, when I was a little older than eleven, we had a general contractor build the shell of the ranch house in Emma where Dad still lives. It looks like a typical Bavarian mountain home: exposed wood beams, white stucco walls, and red tiled roof. He, Nome, and us kids finished the inside ourselves to save money, hand-building six fireplaces with stones we'd helped collect from Aspen Mountain and the Ruedi Reservoir. We stuccoed, laid tile floors, and painted, and, in the process, we learned one of my favorite skills ever: how to swear in German (swearing in English was verboten), acquiring a repertoire that included nearly a hundred words I couldn't use in polite company in Germany today. The experience of building that home and particularly those fireplaces instilled in us a can-do attitude at a very young age and gave us a sense of pride in accomplishing something on our own.

Nome was fierce when it came to academics, and she taught us how to read and study. There are too many stories to tell of nights going over every math problem in our textbooks, falling asleep exhausted over our homework. But when the school had the temerity to suggest to her that I should be kept back a year because I seemed to be intellectually deficient, she refused to accept their assessment. Instead, she chose to believe in my potential. Nome told us we could do anything we set our minds to and that we shouldn't let anyone tell us otherwise. I'm convinced that her deep faith in me is how and why I left high school as valedictorian and eventually went on to the Ivy League for college and to everything else that has happened since.

We were also inculcated with a deep sense of personal responsibility. In seventh grade when I needed a note for an absence from school, Nome wrote one to Mr. Hennington, the principal at the Basalt High School: *Dear Mr. Hennington*, it read. *Please excuse Wally from all absences from now until the time he graduates.*

*Sincerely, Nome Obermeyer.* He laughed when he read it and told me he couldn't accept it. I told him he'd need to talk to my mom. Back home, when I let Nome know what he'd said, she got in the car and drove straight to the school; an hour later, she returned and announced that it was all taken care of. "I asked him how he expected me to raise responsible children if they could not be trusted to know the difference between right and wrong. 'Wally will never do the wrong thing,' I told him. 'He knows the difference, and if he can't be in school for some reason, then it is a good one.'" She was right, though I'm not sure I ever told her about the time I took off for two days to ski in perfect powder with my physics teacher during an excellent snowstorm in Utah. (While there were no repercussions for me about that little excursion, there were for him: He got found out and was fired for his transgression.) Nome had planted an important seed in me that day: Because she believed in my ability to know right from wrong and act accordingly, I started to believe in myself too.

By middle school, Susan had started spending more and more time with us. A second lawsuit had commenced around her custody, and it was determined that she should be with her brothers as much as possible. I was happy with that turn of events as I always worried about her and wanted to protect her. I felt particularly proprietary about my darling sister. She may have suffered most from the divorce and the lack of stability in the family, and at that time she seemed very vulnerable. I would often wake in the morning to find that she had taken her blanket, snuck into my bedroom in the middle of the night, and made a little nest for herself under my bed. I think that vulnerability sometimes caused her to look in the wrong places for guidance. She was always incredibly creative, sensitive, and spirited, always up for a prank, and she hung out with some pretty experimental types during high school. Susan was also always attracted to and loved all animals, particularly horses, and she went on to become a very accomplished equestrian, specializing in long-distance competitions.

Most of us can look back on our growing-up years and see when things really started to shift: My transformational year came when Nome and my dad took me out of school to go with them to Germany. I'd gotten my homework assignments from my teachers in advance, but instead of doing every other problem in my math book, like the teachers at school called for, Nome made sure while we were away that I did every single problem and finished the entire book. To say that she had very high standards would be an understatement. I learned how to learn on that trip and was far ahead academically when I returned, making up for my previous deficit. I also came back from Germany wearing knickers instead of regular pants. I endured a little teasing at first, but soon some of the other kids got knickers too. That would be my first and last time as a fashion trendsetter.

The relationship I built with my German relatives, especially with Uncle Heine, my dad's brother, was life-changing for me. Uncle Heine was very different from Dad: He could sit for hours in his library or on the porch reading, and while he enjoyed hiking, he wasn't driven to be in constant motion like my dad was. Their father, Fritz, was a proud Bavarian and equestrian, always the center of attention on his great white horse leading the parades and festivals in and around Oberstaufen. He was an extremely accomplished artist recognized for his work throughout Europe—among all the family members, we're lucky to have about a hundred of his paintings. During the years when the Nazis were in control, only paintings of flowers were allowed, but thankfully the family was able to hide many of his works under the rafters in their home and they survived the war. But unlike his son Heine, who ran a successful business that my cousin and aunt are still involved with today, Fritz was not a great businessperson. He left the paying of bills up to his industrious wife, Mina. After the war Mina went on to expand her business and started the clothing company that continues to be run by my aunt and cousin in Oberstaufen, Germany, today.

In addition to being an equestrian like his father, Fritz, Uncle Heine was studious and an avid reader. He spoke and read in six languages, which he had learned on his own with books written in those languages. He believed that a complete education must include books that addressed the great ideas essential to a liberal arts education, like *To Kill a Mockingbird* and *A Tale of Two Cities*; I can still recite the opening paragraphs of the latter to this day. While my kids might be surprised to hear this, as they give me grief for only wanting to read what they call "self-help"—and which I think of as "philosophy"—there was a time when all I read was novels. Later, when I was older, Uncle Heine would recommend thinkers like Mortimer Adler, who was one of the editors of Great Books of the Western World and coincidentally part of the founding group of the Aspen Institute and Aspen Ideas. But beyond the books themselves and the intellectual guidance he gave me, Uncle Heine made me feel I was part of a bigger family, one in which I could be more myself—more academic and less dedicated to physical pursuits—and still be an Obermeyer.

Uncle Heine's wife, my beloved Tante Cilly, was pure joy. Although she worked in the family business and still does to this day, she was also dedicated to grace and beauty. When she thought that our studying had carried on long enough and was too intense, she would arrive with a big plate of sugar-dusted cookies and let everyone know it was time for a break. I've never seen a breakfast as extravagant and beautifully presented as Tante Cilly's—five different cheeses, smoked meats, salmon, pastries, Weisswurst, eggs, bacon, fruit, muesli, honeys, jams, and a selection of various butters, all served on matching china with sterling cutlery. Her house is beautiful, full of flowers and sunlight and paintings and artifacts she brought back from their extensive travels to faraway lands. She made me feel cherished and safe. She had infinite patience for my stories and always wanted to know what I was thinking and how she could make my life easier.

I had the most fun with my cousins Klaus and Michael. Klaus was much like his dad, quite serious and studious and in school during the day when I was visiting; his younger brother Michael became my more constant companion even though I was older. We were *freche Buben*—wiseasses—according to our exasperated parents, always up to some naughty caper, whether collecting horse chestnuts at the bottom of the hillside they lived on and throwing them from high up in the tree at passersby or launching paper airplanes off the church balcony at the parishioners below. We found caves in the hillside and squeezed ourselves into them, not really knowing what was on the other side but covering ourselves head to toe with sticky clay mud. We would arrive back from days cavorting in the woods and fields so dirty that Lisbet, who worked for Tante Cilly and Uncle Heine (and still does forty-seven years later), would make us strip down outside and then send us straight to the shower while she dealt with our dirt-encrusted clothes. To this day, Michael and Klaus are two of my best and closest friends.

They say that memory is in the body as well as in the mind, and when I'm back in Oberstaufen, sharing time with my cousins

on the farm, I feel incredibly alive. Helen says that every time
we're there, she understands me more, and maybe it's because
it felt like home to me in a way that Colorado never did. I was
allowed to be a kid on those visits to Germany, while I wasn't
able to be one back on our farm, where there was too much
to do—especially when my dad and Nome were in Europe on
their summer buying trips for Sport, the skiwear business, and
Henry and I were left alone on the farm to tend to everything
and fend for ourselves.

It's hard to imagine in our current climate of helicopter
parenting, in which most parents won't let their children out
of their sight for even a minute, how much unsupervised time
and responsibility we had during those summers. There was
an elderly woman who came a few days a week and dropped
off casseroles, and Mr. Cisco, one of the local policemen, lived
on our road and turned a blind eye to my driving our 1947
Willys Jeep to the local market—provided I stayed within the
speed limits. He knew I was underage, but he also knew we
were on our own. When Henry and I were teenagers, we would
come home from middle school and high school to a long list
of chores, created by Nome, to be accomplished before she and
Dad returned from work—chopping and filling the wood box,
laying the fires, prepping dinner, feeding the animals, shovel-
ing manure into the spreader, irrigating, fencing, and more.
Because I always wanted to be the good boy, I ended up doing
a lot of the chores myself. There was no question we were all
expected to support the growth of Sport, whether by attending
to household duties so our exhausted parents could rest when
they got home, or later by actually working in their offices.

Like many unique and nontraditional upbringings, ours was
imperfect, and yet, through some kind of alchemy, the lack of
traditional parental supervision transformed into wonder. We

spent hours driving farm equipment, which for two young boys was empowering, and when chores were done there was fun. Off hours we could be found building and shooting rockets into the pond (mostly Henry's idea of fun), riding our horses up to the crown and into Old Snowmass, fishing in the rivers. It was a real Huck Finn childhood, so much of it magical, all of it full of the profound beauty of nature in our mountain life. That kind of independence was more common in the West than in more urban and coastal regions, I would later learn, and the world we came from was different then, one where none of our neighbors saw it as neglect, the way they most likely would now.

# EARLY ADVENTURES IN
# ENTREPRENEURSHIP

According to Warren Buffett, one of the best indicators of a successful entrepreneur is how young they are when they start their first business. I started at seven or eight when a friend and I, predictably, set up a lemonade stand in the West End of Aspen. That neighborhood wasn't very busy back then, and, not surprisingly, our sales were pretty pathetic. But when we moved our enterprise over to the Aspen Meadows, where my dad played tennis, everything changed. Our sales picked up dramatically because almost every adult who left the club was hot and sweaty and needed what we conveniently had to offer. Location mattered; lesson learned. Decades later, I would follow that lemonade-stand-next-to-the-tennis-court model when I opened my investment business in Aspen in 1997. So many people had significant liquidity as real estate prices went up, and the community's reputation as a playground for the rich and famous was expanding: Being there would put me in the best position to help all those former and future residents manage their money.

By the time I turned twelve, I had realized that a certain kind of freedom came from financial independence, and I was determined to make my own money from that point on. Part of my drive to do that came from the fact that Dad was notoriously tight with money—having grown up in Germany during the war, he raised us to conserve and not be wasteful. We were taught to keep anything that might be useful in the future, to eat everything put in front of us, and to understand that where a nickel could be saved, a dime had been created. Another part of my drive was the result of Sport Obermeyer being a twenty-four seven focus for all of us: I grew up learning on a cellular level about building and running a business. We all knew our lives depended on the continued growth of Sport. The company was the family. It was the number one priority. And then, for me, there was the fact that "business" always seemed quite exciting and fun. Although we had a constant parade of skiers, models, and ski industry notables coming through our home in those days, it was the numbers that interested me. Dad was becoming a legend. Starting with making his own down-filled parka from a quilt when he first came to Aspen, Klaus's many innovations— including double and flow-fit ski boots, tapered aluminum ski poles, ski breaks, mirrored sunglasses, high-altitude sunscreen, double-lens goggles, traditionally iconic sweaters and ones made from "ski cashmere" (merino wool face, cashmere back), and the kids' I-Grow line with extendable length jackets and pants— were transformative to the ski industry.

I didn't see any reason why I shouldn't start and build a business too.

My first business plan, written out on a yellow legal pad in the summer of 1970 when I was twelve, was something I hoped would appeal to Aspen's local "hippie" population, whom I'd heard was down on industrialized food products and wanted naturally grown, locally produced, and unprocessed food. Having spent a lot of time in Germany on family trips, I knew that the best milk and cream in the world came from Brown Swiss cows and that someone down valley raised them. I also knew that Aspen people would willingly pay premium prices for what they considered high-quality dairy—personally I preferred the pasteurized homogenized version, but I didn't let that get in the way of my business idea. My plan proposed the purchase of two Brown Swiss cows that I would milk twice a day, selling the milk and cream through a kind of store I would set up for the people who wanted to buy natural, unpasteurized, non-homogenized milk and cream.

On my "pitch" day, I hitchhiked up to Aspen, walked into the Bank of Aspen, and asked the teller if I could speak with the president of the bank. Even though I could barely see over the teller's window, she put me through to the secretary, who was either charmed by my youthful cluelessness or entertained by the question. When she buzzed the president in his office, he said, "Well, send him up and let's see what he's got." It must have been a slow day at the bank, but as I would go on to learn throughout my life, sometimes it's just that kind of luck that makes everything possible. Standing in his office, I took out my yellow legal pad and laid out my plan. He listened to me, looked through my numbers, and after nodding a few times and leaning back in his big leather chair, he said, "Congratulations, Wally. You're going to be the proud owner of two Brown Swiss cows." He cosigned the loan, I hitchhiked back home, and I went and bought the cows.

A while later, when Nome and Dad returned from their buying trip, they were surprised but delighted to see my operation in action. I had built two milking stalls in an unused part of the barn, bought refrigerators, and supplied milk bottles that people could take and return, paying for purchases on the honor system. I went on to milk those cows, Silky Milky and Boss, morning and night for the next four years through high school. Smelling like Bag Balm didn't ingratiate me with the girls, but I didn't care. My business was growing, and I was gaining a sense of independence that felt good. After I graduated and started ski patrolling in Aspen, my dad would buy the cows back from me.

He was always very supportive when we kids took the initiative to be creative and entrepreneurial.

To be successful, entrepreneurs know that they need to keep growing, whether it's by expanding on an original idea or sensing when to stop and move on to a new one. I was pretty sure I didn't want to milk cows for the rest of my life, and I knew I wanted to get a job in the ski industry. Snowmass was a ski resort developed in 1967 down valley from Aspen and Aspen Highlands, and it was obvious by the time I graduated in 1974 that it was going to be a great success. With so much development going on then around the base of the mountain for ski-in, ski-out lodging, I saw an opportunity to use the almost twelve thousand dollars I'd saved from my cow business for a down payment on one of the new Crestwood condominiums, which I intended to use solely as a rental property for income. I remember how nervous I was at the closing because I'd had to borrow around thirty thousand dollars, and I had never written checks as large as the three I needed to give to the realtor that day.

The first person I rented it to was a pretty girl—all girls were pretty to an eighteen-year-old boy like me—whose only issue, it seemed, was that she couldn't come up with the first and last month's rent plus a deposit. Enamored and eager to find someone to cover my three-hundred-dollar monthly payments, I told her not to worry about that last month. But at the end of the ski season when she moved out, taking all the furnishings with her—even the dishes—it taught me a great lesson. I could still be understanding and accommodating, but I would need to learn to be a better judge of character if I didn't want to lose my shirt on every deal I made.

Working at Sport Obermeyer as a kid and always being encouraged to think about better and faster ways to do things led to some interesting and funny adventures. One summer, I was tasked, along with Andy Mill, who was among the celebrated ski personalities whom Sport Obermeyer sponsored in those days, with filling bottles with sunscreen. My dad had helped formulate Sportana sunscreen, which was particularly good for cold weather and intense sun and remained a strong seller for many years. We were instructed to use a low-pressure filling mechanism to transfer the product from the fifty-five-gallon drums into the bottles that the lotion was shipped in. That process, however, created air bubbles, which required us to tap down the jar several times while filling each bottle. It was slow and laborious and not fun at all, until we decided to increase the pressure by six or seven times—we were being paid by the number of bottles filled, and this would mean we could increase our revenue by six or seven times. But what seemed like a great idea turned out to be comically disastrous, like that classic scene in *I Love Lucy* where the conveyor belt starts going faster and faster until it eventually overwhelms Lucy and Ethel. Andy and I were working as fast as we could, but we looked like a circus show, our arms flying and both of us laughing so hard we almost ended up with a warehouse covered in sunscreen. Luckily, we were both athletic and quick enough to avert disaster and make it work—well enough that we ended up smiling all the way to the bank.

Another of Sport's innovations was mirrored sunglasses for skiing. Toward the end of the ski season, one of our production batches arrived with a slight defect, and since I was craving some warm weather, I decided to go find some. I hopped in my yellow VW Bug, grabbed the defective glasses, and convinced a friend to go with me to Mexico. After a week or so, we were low on money, so it seemed like the right time for a pop-up store. We laid out a blanket in the main square of Mazatlán, pulled the glasses out of the trunk of my car, and set up shop. Mirrored sunglasses were a coveted commodity at the time, and they sold like hotcakes. Of course, it didn't take long for us to get the attention of *las tiras*, the local Mexican police, and to avoid being put out of business, we "gifted" them each a pair. They sauntered away looking extremely cool, and we kept selling until our inventory was depleted and we had made enough to continue our travels.

One summer, while I was with my parents on one of their buying trips in Europe, we all decided I could travel by myself for a month. I bought a Eurail pass, which was a great deal because the marginal cost of using it was so low. To save more money, I set up my itineraries so that I could sleep on the trains at night and explore during the day. The Eurail pass also included discounted ferry tickets between Norway and Sweden, and one of the ferries had a slot machine that I realized accepted both Norwegian and Swedish crowns. The difference in valuation between the two currencies—10 to 15 percent depending on the exchange rate built into the machine—inspired me to take advantage of the situation: I would ride the ferry back and forth, putting one currency in and getting the other out, exchanging it and making some money. Even at that young age, when I saw an economic opportunity, I had a propensity to try to make use of it because it felt fun and exciting. On my last ferry ride, before I got kicked off, I met a Swedish girl a little older than me who was heading back to her family farm, where the strawberry harvest was about to start. She was amused by my arbitrage experiment, and maybe I mentioned I was low on funds, so she asked if I wanted to come home with her and work. Of course I said yes, and I spent the remainder of my sixteenth summer picking strawberries in the Swedish countryside and dreaming about that beautiful girl whose romantic interest in me amounted to only a sweet pat on the top of the head.

# LESSONS FROM THE FARM

Whenever I ponder tenacity and how it applies to business, I always think about the 4-H Catch-a-Calf Contest. 4-H was central to my growing up in Emma, especially the year I entered one of my lambs in the weeklong 4-H Eagle County Fair, which is a big part of summer in Western Colorado. One of the events was the Catch-a-Calf, and I knew I wanted to give it a try. The competition entails putting a group of nine- to fourteen-year-olds into an arena with a calf; the kid who catches the calf gets to pick a calf from the herd of the sponsor and raise it as a 4-H project for the following year. Just like in football, where only one player can hold or touch the ball at a time, only one kid could hold or touch the calf at a time. When I caught the calf, holding him first by the hoof and then working my way up to his leg and on to his neck, I would not let him go. That calf dragged me top to bottom and side to side around that arena for what seemed like an hour, and by the end I was covered in mud from head to toe. But I had won. I have heard from my parents, who were in the audience, that everyone was amazed by my tenacity. I think I was too.

As the Catch-a-Calf winner, I got to pick a calf from the herd at Strang Ranch. Owner Mike Strang had donated the calf, and he pointed out one he thought had particularly good conformation. "Calfy" became my constant companion. Not only was he beautiful, he was also gentle and friendly and willing to do whatever I asked of him. Calfy was a people pleaser. Not all cows or animals are that way. Just like humans, they're born with personalities and temperaments that stick: Some are ornery and mean from the start, while others only want to cuddle and be loved. Calfy was a cuddler, just like a pet dog, but part of the 4-H experience was coming to understand and accept the fact that cows are not pets—they're raised for milking or for slaughter.

Nome encouraged me to keep meticulous records for the review the following year—we would be judged on who had the best-trained calf, or, by that point, young steer. I learned to track how much money we spent on caring for Calfy, how much food he consumed, and when he got his shots, with Nome impressing upon me the importance of this kind of attention to care and feeding. Farming was a business, and 4-H was teaching me the basics.

Calfy won the grand champion steer competition at the 4-H fair one year after I got him. That meant that the local supermarket had the right to purchase him from me. It was excruciating to let him go, and the money I had earned from making him a winner didn't matter or soften the blow. But I didn't have a choice, and I knew I was expected to be brave. About a month later in the supermarket with Nome, we passed by the meat section and saw a dozen steaks with flags on toothpicks sticking out of them: "Grand Champion Steer." My Calfy. That's when I broke down and cried.

My grand championship win was due to a combination of showmanship of my well-trained steer and my impressive recordkeeping, the latter of which helped me understand the economics of a new venture: the work involved, the money involved, the time involved—skills that would carry through to my adult business endeavors.

The origin story of my notoriously nerdy love of spreadsheets can likely be traced back to the recordkeeping for that 4-H project. Recently my sister, Suzan (she changed the spelling of her name when she became a professional artist), reminded me about some of the more annoying memories of me as her big brother, and my obsession with recordkeeping figured prominently in one of them. She was in 4-H and wanted to graduate from her little pony, Pancho, to a horse we had on the ranch. But 4-H required that she complete some kind of certification before they would let her take on the added responsibility of a big horse, and as I'd learned from Nome about the value of checklists, I'd made Suzan go through every last detail on hers before she submitted the paperwork. It took the entire summer to complete, but by the end of it, she was more than ready for that horse, and I would like to think I taught her some good skills, ones that would be useful to her going forward. Her love for horses certainly endured. The lifelong label of being annoying seems like a small price for our mutual satisfaction.

There's an essential resourcefulness in everything you do on a farm that is applicable in a broader way to all aspects of life, and I think every child should spend at least a year living on one. Nothing is ever thrown away, for instance, and if you walk around any farmyard and look carefully, you'll see how everything is recycled and put to some new use—cow milking station guides look surprisingly like the pipe from an irrigation line; an old tire becomes a planter for early spring vegetable sprouts. That's why most farms are filled with rusted cars and discarded equipment: There's always the chance that some old piece of junk could come in handy down the road.

Our farm was no exception. One summer when my parents were in Europe, I decided to surprise them and make a cover for the pool so that my dad, an avid swimmer, could swim year-round. I used old barn siding for the structure and sheets of plastic to let in the sunlight and keep the water warm; an old door was a perfect fit for the entrance. That heated pool house kept the pool in use all year and lasted a decade.

When I was even younger, there was a train that went from Glenwood Springs to Aspen, which was part of the Denver and Rio Grande Western Railroad. We thought of it as our personal taxi service. Nome would bake pies and give them to the conductor, and in return he ignored the railway rules and would slow the train and let us jump aboard when we were coming or going to Aspen. He would let us ride in the locomotive or in the caboose, then drop us along the track at our favorite fishing holes or anyplace we wanted to explore. The railroad was eventually discontinued, but the tracks and ties remained. A few summers after the train stopped, I started up the backhoe and helped myself to several of the railway ties and rails, which are still holding up foundations and roofs of buildings all around the farm today.

One story I tried to keep hidden from my parents was the time I got our Jeep stuck in the lower wetlands part of the ranch down near the Roaring Fork River. We had a big pile of firewood down there, and one of the chores Nome and Dad had given me to complete before they returned from Europe that summer was to fill the garage with a winter's supply of firewood. Our fires burned almost all winter long; not only did they provide additional heat, but we also used them to smoke bacon inside the chimney and even occasionally to cook delicious roasts. I started the task without taking into consideration how wet the spring had been. First the Jeep got stuck in the muck, and then when I used the tractor to try to pull it out, it promptly got stuck too. To try to fix this disaster, I carried cement blocks down to the bog, thinking I could create a stable enough platform under the tractor to back it out onto dry land. It worked. After dragging nearly one hundred blocks, I got enough traction to pull both the tractor and the Jeep out. Those blocks are still at the bottom of the bog, and it wasn't until recently that my dad realized where that supply of old cement blocks mysteriously disappeared to so long ago.

We think of people—family, friends, colleagues—as having distinct personalities, but, as I learned with my prize-winning calf, animals have them too. A mare I had was a handful, but I still wanted to breed her and raise the foal. When I asked our neighbor about breeding her to his beautiful stallion, he thought about it for a while and eventually agreed—with the condition that I mow his lawn all summer as compensation for the stud fees. I probably spent sixty hours mowing his lawn, all in exchange for the breeding procedure, which couldn't have taken more than two minutes. I did get a beautiful foal, who was much better natured than his mother ever was, so in the end it was well worth it.

Silky Milky, one of our milk cows, was incredibly sweet and compliant (clearly we weren't very inventive when it came to naming our animals), and she'd go along with almost anything we wanted to do with her, including tying an apple on a string to a stick and holding it out in front of her nose, then climbing aboard for a ride. She'd follow that apple wherever we pointed it, and had our legs not become so sore from her backbone (cows aren't as comfortable to ride as horses), we'd have never gotten off. My other cow, Boss, was very ornery, kicking over pails of milk any chance she got. During the fifteen to twenty minutes it took to hand-milk her, I had to be extremely alert, and I had to be vigilant about keeping their udders clean to prevent infection: Milking a cow with mastitis was a fight, as unpleasant for her as it was for me—if not worse, given the kicking and biting. I learned enduring life lessons taking care of animals on the farm. When one of our beef cows went into a difficult labor, the vet made me pick up her prolapsed uterus and put it back inside her. I was only fourteen at the time, and I never took the birth process for granted after that experience.

I'm happy now not to live on a farm. If I think of it in purely economic and numerical terms, the way I was taught years later in business school, the amount of work versus the payout is tough to reconcile—not to mention the allergies I tried to ignore; I live with permanent lung damage to this day from dander-induced asthma. But I wouldn't give up that childhood for anything. I wish everyone could experience what I did. Farming is life and farming is death, and you learn a lot about both. You also learn a lot about hard work and selflessness: Animals need to be fed regardless of weather, homework, or illness; hay needs to be cut and baled when the time is right; crops need to be planted and harvested on their schedule, not on yours. Farming teaches responsibility, compassion, patience, and how to live with the seasons and in peace with the cycles of life. If there are more important lessons than those, I still haven't learned them.

# THE LUCK OF THE SKI LIFT

Nome believed that working and learning was what life was all about—the concept of play less so. On the chalkboard in her family's dining room was one of her dad's favorite expressions: "If you're really good at a sport, that's a sign of a misspent youth." By comparison, one of my father's favorite sayings was "If you're a son of a bitch and you go to a good school, you're just an educated son of a bitch." Despite being educated himself as an aeronautical engineer in Germany before turning skiing into a business, he had a philosophy that included hard work and perseverance, but he also prioritized play. In summer he played tennis almost every lunch break, and in winter, if the snow was good, he grabbed his skis and did a few—or more—laps on the mountain. He didn't have the same appreciation for academic pursuits that his brother and others did. Maybe it was that dissonance in my family's views that led me to take six years off between high school and college. I needed to figure out where I myself fell between those two distant poles of thought.

To say that ski patrolling was something I really wanted to do would be a huge understatement, but I knew that making it onto the patrol would be a stretch: There were no high school students on the patrol. Still, I did everything I could to land one of the coveted positions—a neighbor of ours was the head of Aspen Mountain Ski Patrol, and I would stop by his house about once a week and say, "Just want you to know that I'm really interested in ski patrolling." I think he finally got the message. I was so thrilled when I got my first-aid card and made it through the tryout that the grief I got about my age from the others on the patrol—most of whom were seasoned mountain-man types—felt like a small price to pay to someone who still had braces on. That grief was exacerbated by my relentless drive to do well. Doing well on the ski patrol was predicated on the number of accidents you went on. Needless to say, I volunteered for every single one that I could, and by about midway through my first season, I had been to forty-three wrecks, which didn't endear me to the old-timers, most of whom had only been to a few accidents—or none. I guess you couldn't blame one of them for hiding my skis one day so that I couldn't make it to an accident. It was a bit of a "slow down, kid" warning. I'm sure my over-zealousness was more than a little annoying, but I couldn't help myself; I was in my element. I liked the challenge of figuring out the rescue as much as I enjoyed the skiing.

One of the more exciting calls we got was to rescue a skier who had fallen into an old mining shaft in what are now called the Dumps on Aspen Mountain. Aspen had started as a mining town, and there are still mine shafts all over the surrounding mountains—some of which I've been down in—and they are vast. Locals say the interior of the mountain looks like Swiss cheese, with some of the caverns being so big you could fit the entire Hotel Jerome into them. This poor guy had been skiing the powder in the trees in an area of the mountain that wasn't officially open, and he had fallen headfirst, breaking through into a mine shaft. When I arrived on scene, he was hanging by his bindings headfirst in a shaft that probably dropped two hundred feet. I knew that his bindings could release at any moment and that if they did, he would plummet to his death. I roped on to several trees, called for help, and then got the ropes around his waist, telling him all the while: "For God's sake, stay still."

Luckily, he did, and we got him out of there. Aspen Skiing Company spent the next summer making sure all the mine shafts on Aspen Mountain were sealed.

There were other calls that didn't end well, and those left the most lasting impressions on me. I'm a conservative skier these days, knowing how much fun the sport is while simultaneously being keenly aware of the dangerous consequences of skiing out of control or on unsafe terrain. One of the more fun assignments was being on avalanche patrol, which involved carefully skiing to the top end of where a slide might occur, placing spikes of dynamite connected by one long fuse called a Primacord, then skiing back to a safe zone before—*kaboom*—we blew the whole thing up. The energy of an avalanche is truly something to behold. Nothing stands in the way of Mother Nature when she is ready to express herself. They mostly use 105 mm howitzer guns now to shoot into the snow, but skiing into those avalanche zones back in the day was exhilarating, and it brought back fond memories of all the fun times Henry and I spent blowing things up when we were kids.

After my fourth year of ski patrolling as the patrol's youngest-ever member, I had that been-there, done-that feeling, even though in many ways I had never been happier. Out of the house on my own, away from the chaos, I had an active social life, and in many ways I was living my dream. I was sales repping for our family business, as I had been for the summer and fall seasons during the ski patrol years, and during that time I got my pilot's license. I had always loved flying and flew whenever I could with my dad. My sales territory included Utah, Montana, Wyoming, and part of Idaho, and covering those long distances from Aspen by air made sense. But more than that, it enhanced a sense of freedom and filled me with awe. It was the culmination of all of my aspirations at that time: skiing and flying. I loved sales repping, and I loved flying, but my frustration with our company's inefficient inventory system was growing, and while I had convinced my dad to let me computerize the business, a project I enjoyed and that I'll talk more about later, I was still restless. Again, I had come to a point where I wanted more, though more of what, I still didn't know. I loved skiing, of course, but it wasn't my whole world the way it was for my dad and Klausie. Other things interested me too: economics, working, my belief in the ability to improve society through intellectual thought and discussion. My then girlfriend and I had something we called the Plato Group: Every Saturday, we would have friends and interesting people over for debates, a group that might include the biggest drug dealer we knew, or the sheriff, or a local author. Aspen was, besides being a mecca for skiers and the glamour set, a melting pot of spirited, curious, thinking people, and I was attracted to them, much more than the rest of my family was. I was finally ready to think about college. But when I applied I did not get in.

A lot is written about how childhood adversities can become strengths in adulthood because we learn to work around our challenges, or with them, but luck has a lot to do with how life can turn out too—the luck of being in the right place at the right time, especially when you're at a crossroads. I was about to be lucky again when I found myself occasionally riding the ski lifts with three smart entrepreneurial up-and-comers who were running corporations: Skip Rapp, whom we'd hired at Sport and who had gone to Princeton and then Stanford business school; Whip Jones, who had gone to Harvard; and D. R. C. Brown, who had gone to Yale and now ran the Aspen Skiing Company.

Until then, I'd only heard of Harvard and Yale when Nome's younger brother sang, "I've never been to Harvard / I've never been to Yale / The only place I ever been is the good old county jail." But now, hungry for guidance and direction from people who had in common great educations, I was learning through these friendships about a world I had known nothing about— the Ivy League—and I wanted to be more like them. I was eager and ready to think about college.

I wrote my first applications to Yale, Amherst, and Princeton, the schools I now knew about from my mentors, in a coffee shop in Wyoming while on one of my sales repping trips. I was deferred at Yale and rejected at Princeton and Amherst, and despite my having written the Harvard application in pencil and spilling coffee all over it, they were intrigued enough to defer their decision and asked me to come in for an interview. Maybe it was all the business experience or life experience I had acquired by then, or because I had shaved my beard the morning of the interview, but they let me in. I've always thought that the happiness I experienced when I got that acceptance letter from Harvard was greater than it would have been for an average kid who had applied to college simply as a way to meet family expectations. I can remember the feeling of pure joy and excitement of that day so clearly. When the letter came to the Sport Obermeyer office, I opened it, closed it, and went outside without saying a word to anyone. Then I did a flip into a snowbank. I don't know where the impulse or the physical power to do that flip came from, but it was a literal jump for joy. The memory of the pure elation of that moment, solitary as it was, still makes me cry.

For many people, college is a natural next step in life. But for me and my family, college in general and Harvard in particular was not. My parents had never asked me if I wanted to go or where I would want to go, and my father had stuck to his belief that character and action had more value than formal education. I don't disagree, but in my mind, while a good education shouldn't be overvalued, it shouldn't be devalued either. Many years later, I would learn from Suzan that there was quite a bit of hand-wringing going on about my decision and my parents' fear that their "mountain boy" was going to be corrupted by East Coast liberals—despite the fact that Nome was a product of that very world. I suspect their feelings may also have had something to do with losing a cheap source of labor: I'd been helping the family business and doing a good job for the twenty-five-thousand-dollar salary my dad thought was more than adequate for me then and likely into the future—why did I have to go and ruin a good thing?

I had gone about the application process in a haphazard and spontaneous way—my way—that allowed me to follow my instinctive curiosity to pursue my own interests and passions as they appeared instead of feeling pressured into a prescribed traditional course of action. The advantage of not having had a parental road map drawn for me was that I was forced to draw one for myself. The adversity of having been on my own so much as a child had made it necessary for me to find my own way, and as hard as that was at times, there was freedom in it too. My life was my own. I was now about to find my way to a whole new world where I would figure out what I wanted to do and who I wanted to be.

# NOTES FROM THE OLD COUNTRY

It would be impossible to tell the story of my life without talking about the outsize influence my father has had on me. Klaus Obermeyer is a legend. As I write this, he is 105 and still swims laps in his pool almost every day. He skied until his 103rd year, which means he has pursued his passion for 100 years and is an inspiration to everyone in Aspen who loves skiing and all aspects of mountain life. My dad's story is one of strength and heroism that amazes everyone and one that I'm proud to tell, but he gave me other gifts that go beyond the tale of his survival and escape.

He was born in 1919, just after the end of World War I, in Oberstaufen, a small farming and vacation town in Bavaria in southern Germany. His father, Fritz, was a renowned painter and a well-loved member of the community. Tall, blond, blue-eyed, and handsome, he was Aryan, a word that would later take on a much darker meaning. Riding his beloved white horse, Aster (who would, years later, die the day after Fritz did, something most people never believed was a coincidence), around town every day, talking with all the locals and getting all the gossip, Fritz cut quite a dashing figure. He was proud of his heritage, and he loved to dress up in lederhosen and his traditional *Trachten* jacket and lead the parades in the local festivals.

Klaus's mother, Mina, was Jewish, and she ran the family store. She was equally loved, generous, and warm. When times were tough, the people of Oberstaufen knew they could rely on her to help extend credit for food and supplies. She could always find a spare egg or a slice of lamb for those in trouble, and because she was so beloved, the locals protected her when the Nazis came to power. The Obermeyers represented all that is good in small rural farming towns. They loved their neighbors, they had pride in their heritage, and, over the years, they built a legacy that continues to this day. The very successful Obermeyer Modemarkt run by my cousin Michael and his mom, Cilly, and the various homes they have built and neighborhoods they have maintained are all as evident today when you walk around Oberstaufen as they were when Fritz and Mina were alive.

Klaus's earliest memories are of skiing. He took apart an old orange crate, soaked the boards to make them pliable, then tied the tips back so they would curve upward and slide down the slope like the skis he had seen in advertisements. To his mother's dismay, he nailed his winter boots to the boards and took his first runs down the Staufen. It was pure exhilaration, and freedom, and the beginning of a love affair that would become his life's passion.

Unfortunately, those carefree days of Klaus's early childhood gave way to dark, hungry days in the aftermath of World War I. The Treaty of Versailles crippled the German economy and created tremendous unrest throughout the country. People were literally starving, and the citizens of Oberstaufen were no exception. The economic instability of those years made many Germans vulnerable to the false hopes and lies of the charismatic and extraordinarily dangerous Adolf Hitler. People who had previously had no power—the disillusioned and disenfranchised, the unemployed and often uneducated—were specifically sought out by the Nazis and were suddenly in control. The Brownshirts, the homegrown militia that operated outside the law to frighten and intimidate on behalf of the Nazis, became a scourge: Neighbors spied on each other; children turned on their parents; the kids Klaus and Heine had grown up with, typically the roughest and biggest bullies, now wore the brown uniforms and terrorized the community. The quiet little town Klaus had grown up in became the stuff of fairy-tale nightmares.

My father still remembers the night he and his parents and Heine were listening to Voice of America, then banned by the Nazis, and quickly put a pillow over the radio, turned down the volume, and crouched near the floor, watching in horrified silence as a microphone from a Nazi spy slid by the second-story window of their house on Immenstädter Straße. Klaus and Heine joined a group of concerned citizens who would meet in a small mountainside hut to try to figure out ways to subvert the new infrastructure being imposed by this cruel regime. We have since visited the foundation of that hut on the Hochgrat where those meetings took place, and we understood the desperation they must have all felt to be willing to take such big risks.

Usefulness to the new regime was one of the dividing lines between who would survive and who would not. Klaus had an aptitude for engineering, and in 1934, at age sixteen, he was recruited to work in an aeronautical engineering factory in Munich. Heine, like their father, was more of an academic. When the Nazis took over, Heine was classified as *Mischling* (a person of mixed race) and sent to a work camp in Sitzendorf, which, thankfully, was not an extermination camp. But word had spread that the Obermeyer boys were meeting surreptitiously and were not supportive of the new regime, and while Klaus's abilities as an engineer were valuable to the Nazis and thus protected him, there was no guarantee that would last. Eventually, his luck, like that of so many others during this time, would run out.

That day came when Klaus was told by his boss that he needed to flee because they had just received word that the Gestapo were coming to pick him up. There is a story, uncorroborated, about an altercation with a guard during that hurried trip to escape back to Oberstaufen, which may or may not have ended with "someone's" death; for Klaus to have made it meant that someone else did not. Whatever the exact details of that situation actually were, he took his skis—real ones by this point, not homemade orange-crate slats—and headed to the mountains: His intention was to try to ski over the border to safety in Switzerland. He waited there in that same hut on the Hochgrat where he'd met with his resistance group, and several days later, when the guards had moved off the borders of Liechtenstein and Switzerland, he made a break. But he had miscalculated. *"Halt oder ich schieße!"* the guards shouted. *Halt or I'll shoot!* Klaus turned and skied back to where he had come from in Germany and was shot in the back.

Somehow, he managed to keep skiing into the woods, until he went over a cliff, breaking his femur in the fall. Certain that he had not survived, the soldiers gave up their pursuit, and once they were gone, he crafted a sled from his skis and pulled himself to the bottom of a hill into a small town on the border. From there he was taken to the local clinic, which was run by a group of nuns, but since he didn't know if he could trust them, he only said that he'd broken his leg while skiing. Only when he felt he could trust one of the nuns did he reveal that he had also been shot. She advised him to remain quiet until the night shift, when a neutral doctor could perform the surgery to extract the bullet. Back then, a broken leg was put in traction, which would keep a patient in bed for months. During the time that Klaus was recovering, the terrible war finally came to an end. Realizing that the Americans were coming to free Germany, he handwrote a small English-German dictionary from his hospital bed, which turned out to be so useful to everyone on both sides that it went on to have three or four printings before the established dictionary companies got involved. He used the money he earned from the sale of those dictionaries to buy a ticket on the first ship he could find to America. He had seen all he wanted of Germany.

Leaving his mom and dad and brother, Heine, Klaus took his ski clothes and some supplies and set sail. The details of his departure had always been a bit fuzzy until recently, when I hired a superb lawyer, Ellen von Geyso, who is licensed in Germany and America. She helped me dig up all the travel manifests and documentation of Nazi persecution, which became the basis of the successful reestablishment of my father's German citizenship and thus dual citizenship for me, my brother and sister, and my daughter Natalie, this past October 2024, seventy-seven years after he left. Over all these years, he had retained and shared with us so much of the good of his childhood while rejecting the bad—most of my nieces and nephews are quite proficient in German, particularly the Bavarian dialect, and I have a nephew, Karl, who is superb on the accordion and can yodel better than most Germans. For most of his life, Dad had not wanted to reinstate his citizenship, but as he aged and as he saw the same autocratic trends developing in his newly adopted country, he mellowed on the idea. His desire for all of us to retain that deep connection to his home country overcame his anger about how it had almost been ruined during those dark and painful times.

THE CHOICE OF PERCEPTION

One morning during my ski patrol days, I went to the Wiener-stube, a German-themed restaurant just outside Aspen where the locals enjoyed eggs Benedict and pancakes before heading to the slopes. Dad held court at the same table every morning and was a fixture there, always sipping his Viennese *Kaffee mit Schlag*, and that day, when a tourist started to complain about the fact that it was a gray day, Dad dismissed him with a wave. "Maybe," he said. "But above those clouds the sun is shining." Then we all laughed and got up and enjoyed another great day on the slopes because, as Dad also always said, "A day without skiing is a day you can never get back."

Bavaria is the land of Oktoberfest, Hofbräuhaus, and alpenhorns; of accordions and yodeling; of dirndls and lederhosen. It's the land of the Black Forest; of open fields full of flowers and cowbells ringing; of red-roofed, white-stuccoed, timbered houses with richly patterned painted shutters and window boxes overflowing with geraniums; and of the Neuschwanstein Castle, made famous by Disney. No wonder we call it *Schlaraffenland*—fairyland. My father raised us with a love of our German heritage and all the positive aspects of its culture—particularly of Bavarian history and life—and he has a joke and a song for every circumstance. We know them by heart, and we know them in the Bavarian dialect, which is so much its own that although I speak fluent Bayerische I often can't understand haute German when I'm visiting other parts of the country.

When I was in danger of getting a bad grade in my German classes in college, I could rely on softening up my teacher by pulling out one of the jokes from Dad's repertoire.

Unlike their countrymen to the north, Bavarians are joyful, fun loving, and very funny. They're also all about simplicity and practicality. One typical funny story that illustrates these traits is about a Prussian who goes to a beer hall in Munich for *Bierrettich*—beer radish. A Bavarian sitting nearby wants to salt his beer radish, but his salt shaker has gotten wet and the salt won't come out. He tries the salt shaker next to it, and when the salt in that one is stuck too, he pushes the radish away and just has his beer. The Prussian looks at him, grabs a toothpick out of the toothpick jar, and pokes the holes in the salt shaker to clear away the damp salt. When he hands the salt shaker back to the Bavarian so he can salt his radish, the Bavarian says, "Ah, these darn Prussians, with their technological superiority."

The Germans, like many of their European neighbors, inherited a countryside shaped by farming principles from the Middle Ages. The homes are human-sized and concentrated in small villages, and the seemingly endless and undeveloped land between towns is a gift. Hiking and skiing are national pastimes, and people have a deep and abiding love of the outdoors and exercise. My dad embodies the essence of this uniquely European heritage. I remember once asking him if he ever got bored driving from Emma to Aspen, which with traffic can be a forty-minute commute. "No, Wally!" he said. "The mountains and sky and flowers and fields—they are so beautiful and so different every day." When asked about a day of skiing, he'll tell you how the trees look like little gnomes with their hats of snow.

My father's unwavering optimism is immediately apparent to anyone who meets him, and more than anything else, I think, it is what defines him. I've always imagined that such unshakeable positivity came from the joy he must have felt most days for his good luck in escaping his dark past and making it to the country that gave him success, freedom, and access to another range of majestic mountains and all they had to offer. This positive philosophy runs deeply through Sport Obermeyer's corporate ethos. One of their marketing maxims is "There is no such thing as bad weather, just wrong clothing." Another is "Skiing is like being given a pair of wings so you can fly down the mountain." Last fall, I drove up to his house to visit him, and when I arrived, I found him asleep in the sun on the patio. A deer was nuzzling him, and I'm sure it was as alarmed as all of us were to see him so still—he's always been so active, in constant motion. But that day, he was simply completely relaxed and happy on his farm, amid the apple and apricot and plum trees, where there is always a herd of deer, and the chickens are pecking and the cat is purring, and life is beautiful and magical and fairylike. *Schlaraffenland*, indeed.

My father was not perfect. He would always prefer to sit next to a pretty girl on the chairlift than sit with us kids, and we all learned to ski incredibly fast from an early age because if we were not at the lift when he got there, we would not be taking the next run with him. Despite it all, or perhaps because of it, there isn't a day that goes by without something he taught me coming to mind. I credit him for having a belief in all of us, his four children who had very different personalities, for trying to bring out the best in us and allowing us to flourish in the things we were good at. His optimism and devotion to the customers he has served all these years is the lens through which I make every decision and try to solve every problem. His wisdom and

the unconventional way he delivered it to me were wings that
have allowed me to fly down whatever mountain in life I've ever
been on.

# GOING EAST

On a clear September afternoon in 1980, I drove a U-Haul truck down Commonwealth Avenue in Boston and parked on the corner of Fairfield Street in the Back Bay. Out of that U-Haul I rolled my yellow VW Bug and my Honda 90 motorcycle, and then carried books, clothes, and a small arsenal of hunting rifles and shotguns up to the third floor of the brownstone where I had rented an apartment with my girlfriend, Janine, who was going to start at Boston College. Not exactly the way most of my Harvard freshman class of 1984 was arriving that afternoon to start their four years in Cambridge. Transporting guns illegally over state lines was just the first of many things I realized I needed to rethink now that I was living outside Colorado.

On campus, I watched excited parents lead the way to the Harvard Coop, where their credit cards paid for their children's books and supplies. It hadn't occurred to me that parents did that kind of thing: helping shop for bedding or household items for a new college dorm room or apartment. It also hadn't occurred to me to get someone to help me pick my classes and teachers, the way many of the other students had. Nor had anyone explained that by living off campus, I would miss out on the bonding experience of Harvard Yard or the significance of the various clubs. I did not realize that many of my classmates had arrived in search of meaningful social connections as much as top professors. It became obvious from my first moments in

Cambridge that I had a lot more to learn there than the teachings of E. O. Wilson and Larry Summers. All I knew was that I was paying for my own education, and I was there to learn. I intended to take advantage of everything the institution had to offer—or try to, anyway. Recently, an old college classmate called and told me that I was his "hero" at Harvard because I was the one who knew how much every class cost, and how much every minute in class cost. "You were paying for your own education," he said. "It would never have occurred to me to think about it in those terms, and you valued our time there in a way I have not until recently."

I knew from day one that I wanted to be an economics major. I sensed there was a huge amount of tangible good that could come from well-conceived financial systems, and I wanted to understand in depth how society could be organized to maximize economic well-being for the larger good. I wanted to understand the flow of capital and the various structures for harnessing it. I was interested in the nuances in the difference between public and private interest. I wanted to learn more about the philosophy of Adam Smith, even as I wondered whether he had fully taken into consideration negative externalities like the cost to society of pollution or chemical waste—not to mention positive externalities, like how education affects societal outcomes. I was eager to learn more from economic philosophers I had not yet studied: Hume, Locke, Mill, Galbraith, Friedman, and others.

Years later, I would attend a Berkshire Hathaway meeting and ask a question pertaining to this very topic. "Warren and Charlie," I said (the meeting was videotaped), "you two have demonstrated great talent in private-sector capital allocation and shown the world the power of excellence in this area. Do you think there's a similar opportunity for outstanding capital allocation in the public sector, at both the state and federal levels? And if so, what approach and/or changes would you suggest for society to achieve these benefits?" It was a tough question, and I was disappointed that they didn't try to dig in and answer it, but it was the wrong forum for such a discussion since we were there for their company annual meeting. I'd love the opportunity to sit down with Warren and pose the question again because it's so important to think about using economic principles to improve society.

I've always felt that with the privilege of a good education comes the responsibility to use it well. If you get to go to a good school, how can you best use that education in ways that benefit more of society? I think, by and large, that most people do use their education for the greater good—especially those in the medical and public health sector, as well as those working to solve and reverse social, environmental, and climate change problems. I think that society's investment in education gives a big return. It's popular now to criticize the financial industry and corporate America for putting profitability above societal needs, but as naive as it may seem, I still believe that most people running businesses are motivated to make people's lives better. There is no doubt that greed and quarter-to-quarter earnings have encouraged some very negative outcomes for society, but I believe that understanding economics is an essential skill in making the world a better place.

During the years I was ski patrolling, I had taken summer classes at the University of Colorado Boulder in macro- and microeconomics. While I was good at math, once I got to Harvard, I quickly realized that my almost quaint Basalt High

School trigonometry and algebra had not prepared me to compete with my peers who had graduated from places like Andover and Exeter. Instead, I was placed in a remedial math class for my freshman year, and when I took Calculus 1 and 2 in subsequent semesters, I found them challenging. In fact, most of my first two years felt like racing to catch up, which required putting in twice the effort of many of my classmates. But I loved to study and learn, so working hard never felt like a burden. Remember, I was six years older than most of my classmates, and I did not need to spend my freshman year breaking away from the constraints of living at home and parental oversight. I was there to learn, and I did not feel put upon in the least by the rigor of the academic challenges placed on me by my professors. If anything, I felt privileged to be there at all.

When I got to college, I couldn't believe my good luck. Here were a seemingly infinite number of young people, most of whom shared my thirst for knowledge. Everyone was bright and wanted to learn, and if you happened to get an answer right on the test that others missed, people wanted to know how you'd figured it out. You were encouraged to learn and to study, and it was popular to be good at whatever your major was. It was a totally uplifting environment and experience compared to being at Basalt High School, where my classmates had put up with me for being uncool for getting good grades. I'd had to figure out how to navigate between loving to learn and wanting to please my teachers while not completely alienating my peers.

Straddling that line hadn't been easy, and I was often bullied and ostracized. Part of what got me through that time without being completely destroyed by my peers was my love of explosives. While I was, as I mentioned, valedictorian of my high school class, there was no way the principal was going to trust me with that graduation speech; he wanted to see it first.

Twenty minutes before my meeting with him to go over the contents of my speech, I lit the fuse to a chain of M-80 firecrackers that I'd rigged on the flat roof above his office. When all hell broke loose, he jumped up and ran to the door. "Come with me, Wally! Help me catch those damn kids!" Little did he know that the nerd sitting next to him in his office was the true culprit and mastermind of the prank. But those antics got me enough cred with the bullies that they mostly left me alone.

By the beginning of my sophomore year, my relationship with Janine had ended and I knew I wanted to spend more time on campus with some of the people I had met in my classes. That September, when I moved into Lowell House and joined the Fly Club, my social life expanded. There I met Keith Rogal, who came from the nearby town of Weston. He invited me to spend holidays with him, and I felt like part of his family during the six years I would spend in Boston. Bruce Holley and my crewmate Jamie O'Donnell also became great friends through the Fly. Another classmate at Lowell House was Amy Chua, who would go on to write *Battle Hymn of the Tiger Mother* and set an impossibly high standard for parents who wanted their kids to follow them to these elite schools. We shared many fun evenings at the Fly in what we thought were elegant surroundings, unwinding from the rigor of our classes and the pressures of college life.

Even more challenging in Cambridge than academics was parking. As a club member, I got a space in their lot right near the entrance to Lowell, a spot even more coveted than the one our headmaster had. This lucky break gave me an aura of mystique among my classmates. Who was this guy from Aspen? Was he trying to hide great wealth by parking his ancient, battered

VW Bug in such a highly visible spot? I may have looked like just another rich undergraduate with excellent connections in the parking office, but I wasn't that at all. I was just an older student who had driven myself east and occasionally spent time on my giant computer terminal and 1200-baud modem, relics from computerizing Sport Obermeyer's inventory system, a project that I was still working on. No matter what I may have appeared to be on the outside, I was still full nerd on the inside.

In later years, I came to learn that I wasn't the only one who felt out of my depth at Harvard. It was a congregation of extremely talented people, and for many of us, it was the first time we were not the standouts and the tops of our class; we all had to work, and we were all challenged. It would be a rare and likely narcissistic person who did not at one time or another feel that they did not belong. But that was one of the most valuable lessons I learned—not to give up when confronted with people smarter and more connected than I was. Instead, I would double down, figure out how and why others were succeeding where I wasn't, and try to emulate their best characteristics. And I would study harder.

There had always been a part of me that was looking for guidance, for mentors, for a sense of connectedness to family. Of course I had a family, one that I loved deeply and that had given me a lot of foundational knowledge about skiing, farm life, entrepreneurship, and surviving independently—everything that made me who I was and who I still am today—but when I got to college, I learned that other families did things differently from mine, that many people had grown up with a sort of safety net or webbing—emotional support—from parents who guided and advised them on decisions, to ensure that their path forward into the future was visible and intentional. I'd never had that kind of guidance, and I didn't have it now. As if on cue, like Nome appearing in my life out of nowhere and providing a guiding light at a time I needed it most, like the ski lift mentors I'd crossed paths with in Aspen, new people once again would help me find my way through my undergraduate years.

My first roommate, Jeff, for instance, would spend hours on the phone with his parents, talking about what classes he should take and having strategic discussions and conversations that helped guide him through his undergraduate years and into Harvard Law School, and I know that some of what I overheard must have rubbed off on me. Keith's family practically adopted me, always inviting me for holidays—especially Thanksgiving. The Rogal household was always open, and it was a wonderfully warm and emotionally supportive touchstone for me during those years.

But it was Bill Patterson and his family who would later have the greatest positive effect on me. Bill was the other student from Colorado in our class. We were both rowing crew, having been recruited as strong farm boys by the freshman coach. Bill was quite a bit more sophisticated than I was, but we hit it off and became fast friends. One day on the way back from the boathouse, when I was really struggling with my classes, I wondered aloud whether I would be able to continue with crew, afraid that my grades would suffer if I did. We walked in silence until Bill stopped and looked at me. "You know, Wally," he said, "I'd like to think a truly great person could do both." I have thought about that moment countless times since; in many ways, I would say it informed who I am today. I wanted to be a person worthy of that praise and worthy of the admiration of someone I respected as much as I respected Bill.

It was Bill's father who would become a lifelong mentor to me, advising and supporting me in ways I had always craved. Bill and his younger brother, Tom, were both raised in Grand Junction, Colorado. Their dad, Dr. Patterson, was an orthopedic surgeon, a voracious reader, a superb outdoorsman, and a great conservationist. He was also a very successful investor. To this day, I consider the Patterson men some of the finest I have ever known and the most positive influences in my life. As far as I could tell, Dr. Patterson—Bill Senior—knew everything about everything. He was savvy and, in the quietest, most unassuming way, he knew how to gently steer his kids toward success. I don't know how he learned to navigate the world of East Coast elite schools and life since he didn't come from that world himself— born in Belfast, Northern Ireland, he grew up in Columbus, Ohio, and went to both college and medical school at Ohio State University before moving west. But he did learn, and he helped all his kids find their way. Both boys went on to have phenomenally successful careers and great, enduring friendships, and they became upstanding citizens just like their dad.

In many ways, Tom Patterson and I were more alike than young Bill and I were—we would become fast friends when he came to Harvard while I was in business school, but by then we had already spent lots of time hiking and skiing in the mountains of Colorado when we were all back home. Tom also helped me one summer when I was scouting locations for the hydroelectric facility I would go on to build a few years later. Maybe to become closer to Dr. Patterson or to be more like Bill and Tom, I went on to marry their sister. But, like so many things in life that look too good to be true, that seemingly perfect plot twist didn't work out the way any of us imagined it would. A story for another day.

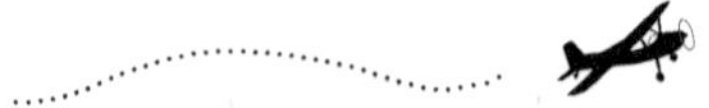

# CREW

Being a student wasn't all library, all the time, though, and because I missed my physical life, I knew I needed an outlet for that. Enter crew. I had no clue that rowing crew was considered an Ivy League badge of honor. Trying to decide between two sports that I found intriguing, fencing and crew, was not as hard as it turned out: The appeal of being outside on the water won out.

I made the lightweight team freshman year, and my crewmates became most of my closest friends while I was in college. Many of them still are to this day: Jamie O'Donnell (from the Fly Club), John Stevenson, Bard Cosman, Albert Léger, Mike Aronow, Pat Bennett, Phil Talbert, Justin Kermond, Edd Fleming, Bill Patterson, and our coxswain, Mike Phillips. Mike became one of the best coxes in the league, and he led us to many great victories with his unique knack for knowing when to ask more of us and when to let us go. Bob Leahey was our superb freshman coach, whom I simultaneously admired and was terrified by. He was tough, and a big part of his job was to weed out those who wanted to say they rowed crew from those who would go on to actually do it. Luckily, he did not weed me out.

I weighed about 165 pounds in freshman year, and to make weight at Friday's weigh-in before race day, I had to get to somewhere between 152 and 155. The freshman lightweight eight-man boat had to average 150 pounds across all the team members; the heaviest person could not be over 155 pounds. I would have recurrent nightmares about being in an ice cream shop and Bob seeing me and yelling at me in front of everyone. I yo-yoed up and down all year, often resorting to wearing parkas in the steam room and starving myself on Thursdays and Fridays. Jamie reminded me recently that on Fridays, which was weigh-in day before our Saturday races, the coach would order Fribbles—rich milkshakes from Friendly's, a regional burger joint—and hand them to us as we stepped off the scale. He said he was amazed at how quickly I gulped down that cold ice cream.

Bruce Beall, our varsity coach, would go on to compete in the quadruple sculls in the 1984 Olympics, but not before helping us achieve a great run of wins. He was a true inspiration. Bill Patterson and Edd Fleming were our captains senior year, when we missed going to the Henley Royal Regatta by two-tenths of a second. We did, however, because of our record, earn a spot to compete in the Dragon Boat Festival in Hong Kong that spring. Word got out in Cambridge about the coveted invitation, and a call was made to the coach from someone high up at Jordan Marsh, one of the better-known department stores in Boston. They had a dragon boat that had once been used for a Hong Kong–related promotion. Jamie and a few other teammates rented a tractor trailer and drove to the location where the dragon boat was sitting in a field. It was no small feat getting it onto the trailer or dragging it into Newell Boathouse and launching it into the Charles River—dragon boats are about forty feet long and weigh around eight hundred pounds. After all that effort, our reward was surprising: The boat sank like a stone.

We probably should have taken that as a premonition, but though we were dismayed, we were undeterred. Harry Parker, the heavyweight coach, who had been observing from the side-lines, strolled out onto the dock to give us a little reassurance: "Don't worry guys, she's just really dry. The wood will rehy-drate, she'll resurface, and you'll be fine." He was right: A few days later, when the boat floated to the surface, we bailed her out, and she was fine. But just to make sure, we hired a Taoist priest who blessed her eyes. We attracted a lot of attention as we floated along the Charles, learning to paddle rather than row, and becoming quite proficient at it.

The problem was that the race was scheduled to take place at the same time as our graduation, which most of my varsity teammates wanted to attend. The ceremony didn't seem like a big deal to me compared to rowing in Hong Kong's Victo-ria Harbor—especially since I doubted that Nome and my dad would even come for the ceremony. In the end, four seniors went on the trip: Albert, Jamie, Justin, and me. Bob Leahey came as our coach and Dudley Herschbach accompanied us as chaperone. Dudley later went on to win the Nobel Prize in Chemistry, a fact that will become important shortly. An unfortunate late predicament, however, was that while practic-ing one day and horsing around, our coxswain fell and broke his leg, so we left for Hong Kong with a cox who had almost no experience.

We reached Hong Kong and were amazed by the spectacle. Dragon boat races are a big deal, and it seemed the entire pop-ulation of the city was on the shoreline cheering for their teams. The boats are colorful and elaborate and the competitors fierce. To ready the harbor for race day, ships were strategically placed at the mouth of the harbor to deter waves and maybe wind. Well, we took off with our new cox into the current and almost immediately started drifting sideways. Turning one of those boats once they get going the wrong direction is like turning a cargo ship. Once we got off balance, the rough water and wind caught us sideways, and we capsized and sank. I remember surfacing and breaststroking toward our rescue boat, pushing away a dead rat in the process. Victoria Harbor was not water you wanted to swim in back in 1984, and no one wanted to be around you if you did: We were not welcomed in the hotel pool where we quickly retreated, hoping the chlorine would counteract the bacteria from the raw sewage being pumped into the harbor.

Prior to our debacle, we'd watched our Shenzhen competitors with intrigue and curiosity as they drank what appeared to be a secret potion before each practice session. They'd bite the top off a glass vial filled with a yellow liquid and then hop in their boats and paddle at what seemed to be two hundred strokes a minute. One of our teammates drew the short straw and was tasked with stealing a vial and giving it to our chaperone, the aforementioned future Nobel laureate Dudley, for inspection. The next morning, we eagerly awaited his analysis of this mysterious liquid, wondering if we, too, could make our own concoction to ensure our success. At the breakfast table Dudley announced his findings: The secret potion was nothing other than honey.

For those of you keeping score at home, these were our lightweight team's standings:

    1981: 3–3, Captain Jeff MacMillan
    1982: 5–1, Captain Ethan Goldings
    1983: 3–3, Captain Jess I. Parks
    1984: 4–2, Captains Bill Patterson and Harold Fleming

And in case you're wondering whether I continued rowing while I was in business school, I did. Here's part of an article that ran in *The Harvard Crimson* in October 1985, about three graduate school boats, including mine, that rowed in the Head of the Charles Regatta that year:

Among the hundreds of club boats entered in the Head each year are several crews with grander connections to Harvard. Some are made up in part or entirely by ex-Harvard rowers. Others, such as the Business School boat, maintain direct ties with the University.

This year, three such special "other" Harvard boats are entered in the Head: the Business School crew, the "Alte Achter," and the "Rude and Smooth."

These club crews serve all kinds of rowers—from former Olympians dedicated to maintaining their skills to less proficient but equally fanatic oarsmen who simply want to relive some of the excitement of their college careers.

While these boats probably won't grab any headlines by winning races, they're deserving of a second look because of their unique backgrounds.

Take the Harvard Business School boat, for starters. It's the easiest one to spot—just look for the dollar signs on the oars.

The B-School Boat Club is a fixture of the Head, having competed in the last eight. The Club is entered in the men's lightweight eight division and is seeded 38th.

Everyone in Captain Wally Obermeyer's boat is an experienced oarsman, among its members are products of the Harvard, Yale, and Princeton rowing programs.

According to Obermeyer, "We miss college rowing. We're all experienced oarsmen and women who love rowing and want to continue it in graduate school."

As one would expect from a team of businessmen, the eight

rowers had to survive a selection process to earn a seat on the boat. "It was sort of a natural selection," Obermeyer said. "There's a growing interest in rowing at the Business School, so many people wanted to be on this boat."

That number steadily dwindled to its present size, though. "We've been working out at Weld boathouse since it opened this year, at 6:15 in the morning, five days a week. The rowers who've stuck with us are pretty serious. It takes a lot of persistence to get up every morning and work out."

Although serious, the B-School crew realizes it isn't a threat to younger competition. Obermeyer commented, "Due to the time pressures of graduate school and the lack of coaching, we realize that we can't be competitive with college rowing teams. But we try to reach as high a level as possible."

And Obermeyer claims they aren't bothered by the lack of prize money. "When we row, we don't think of money."*

I typically rowed in position five or seven, which are two of the four seats often referred to as the powerhouse seats. Jamie had my back—literally and metaphorically. As teammates, we knew we could count on each other for anything, and he's still there to this day, ready to help me in any way he can. From time to time when we reached that state of flow and near-perfect synchronization called "swing," it felt like we were one, connected to each other and united by a single goal and purpose. Those feelings of deep trust and respect have never gone away, and I have only occasionally felt similarly since. In 2016, I had the idea that it would be great to get the team together again, and when I reached out to see if anyone would be interested in doing

* *The Harvard Crimson*, "From Alte Achter to the Rude and Smooth," October 19, 1985.

a five-day biking and camping trip in Moab, Utah, along the White Rim Trail, every single guy came (with the exception of Albert, who was coaching at Exeter and couldn't get away). We set up our chairs next to the campfire in the same order that we had rowed in, and we were right back in swing.

When you row six or seven days a week, through rain, snow, ice, and wind, with a group of eight people—your team—you can't help but build a deep well of respect and admiration for them. The camaraderie, commitment, and teamwork I experienced through crew taught me life lessons that would go well beyond the Charles River and apply long after I left Cambridge.

# HARVARD BUSINESS SCHOOL

As if making up for lost time, I applied to Harvard Business School during my senior year of college, and, again, when my acceptance came, I was incredibly happy—that is, once I retrieved the packet that my roommate had hidden: Teasing me seemed like fun, since it was a very thick packet, so he knew it was good news.

The entering class of HBS is divided into sections, usually about ninety students, who function as a close cohort and tend to form study groups to help manage the first year's Required Curriculum. My year was the first time students were issued computers that came with a two-wheeler to drag them around campus. It's hard to believe technology has changed so much in what feels like such a short time. As always, I was ready to learn, excited to see Excel for the first time, and looking forward to all the technical skills I would acquire. The head of my section was a wonderful professor named Jan Hammond, who had recently come to HBS from MIT. She would become, and remain, a close friend, especially a few years after I graduated and we worked together with Marshall Fisher on the Sport Obermeyer supply chain case study, which I'll talk more about later. About fifteen years ago, we had lunch with her in Cambridge, during a time when my stepdaughter was very concerned about her grades. Jan told her not to worry about her grades. "It turns out that the A students stay in academia, and the B students end up working for the C students," she said. Jan was very practical about academia and loved the students without ever adopting that Harvard grandiosity that many of the professors suffered from.

As many people know, the curriculum at **HBS** is taught entirely through the case study method, which means that students are given a real-world business problem and then asked, with limited information and without knowing how the actual situation turned out, how they would solve it. Typically, we would have to read two to three case studies a day; with five classes, this meant we were responsible for reading between ten and fifteen a week. We knew we had to be ready to be called on by our professors and prepared to demonstrate our proficiency in the material. Most times I didn't know exactly what I would say, what case I would make to solve that particular problem, which likely had multiple solutions. I found this perversely fun and infinitely interesting. While I already had some business experience and knew there were always multiple ways to approach business dilemmas, here, being asked to make a case without having to suffer real world consequences, I could be more creative and have more fun with the idea of problem solving. Because I didn't know ahead of time that the seat you sit in on the first day of class becomes your permanent one for the rest of the semester, I arrived on time to my first class and found, to my surprise, that every seat was taken with the exception of those in the front row, "the worm deck." But classmates who thought they could avoid being called on by sitting in the seats at the back of the classroom, known as the "sky deck," found out that came with a different set of problems: Professors generally had a negative opinion of sky deck students and tended to pick on them more.

My first day of classes at HBS was Jan Hammond's first teaching day, and she had been advised that to control her nerves she should pick one student to focus on and not let herself be intimidated by the rest of the large, eager class. The student she chose was me, and Jan and I have shared a wonderful friendship ever since. By the numbers, the odds of getting called on in each class weren't that high—each student had maybe a one-third chance of being asked to open over the course of the semester. But during my second year when I was taking an international development class with Professor James Austin, I remember him calling on one student three classes in a row, each time a disaster, since the student thought there was no way he'd be called on a second time, let alone a third.

While everyone else was looking at companies to apply to after college, and especially after graduate school, I took another route. My way of doing things was just different from the way most people did them. I rarely followed the rules, not because I was particularly antiestablishment, but because I often didn't know what those rules were. Just as I'd had no idea about colleges when I was applying, as I was finishing up business school, I had no sense of New York: Goldman Sachs, JP Morgan, Chase—all these companies meant nothing to me. I had no sense of them the way my friends did, likely having heard about them at home while growing up. There were the people who wanted to go into consulting, which appeared to be a kind of superhighway to success, and there were other people who wanted to go into investment banking. The people who were deep into consulting and investment banking were not ones I was well acquainted with. The only reason I was even thinking about going through the interview process was that everybody else was doing it. For me, it was less about being competitive for whatever jobs were being offered and more a sense that it must be a good thing to do if everybody else was going. As always, curiosity led me more than a clear sense of ambition did.

On the day of my Goldman Sachs interview, I drove my VW Bug to the downtown hotel where the meetings with HBS graduates were being held. I'll skip the details about how VW heaters at that time basically just blew hot air through some manifolds in the engine, which was in the trunk, and skip to the part about how the cable that controlled the heating system in my car had broken—which meant that the heat in my car was always on. You could not turn it off. I don't remember what I was wearing that day for my interview—likely a suit that I'd bought used at Keezer's in Cambridge, the oldest secondhand clothing store in the country, where most Harvard students shopped and where JFK allegedly sold his clothes at the end of every semester— but I do remember that I was hurrying from whatever my last class was to the garage at the business school where I was lucky enough to have a space.

When I got to my car, I set the heavy stack of books I'd been carrying on the back seat. The car battery of the VW was under that seat, and in my car, the battery was shielded by some cloth, a layer of Aspen wood shavings, and another layer of vinyl. The problem was that all that "shielding" had disintegrated enough that the weight of the books caused the battery terminals to hit the springs in the seat and start sparking, lighting the seat on fire. Fortunately, since it was open air and concrete, the parking garage itself wasn't at risk of catching fire, so once I stopped the car, pulled the seat out onto the cement, and tamped the flames down, I was on my way. Having a car fire right before my first important interview and arriving late, smelling like smoke, with my glasses singed, was not how I'd planned to impress the Goldman Sachs people and the other thirty or so corporate recruiters there. Even I knew that was not what the get-ahead game plan looked like.

Despite my comically bad entrance, when all was said and done—when the interview and small talk over drinks and dinner were over—the basic issue with me remained: I was an outsider. An outsider who had simply done too many things—from ski patrolling to sales repping to computerizing my dad's business to working with Henry on some engineering projects—to make me a clear and obvious candidate for the kind of jobs they were filling. My background and experience may have been intriguing when I'd applied to college, and it was likely also intriguing to the companies I was interviewing with now—not in a bad way, but in a way that would have been risky for somebody to hire me. They sensed that I would eventually want to leave to do my own thing, and I even remember one of the recruiters saying, "Well, you'll probably go back into your family business, right?" to which I replied, "Yes!"

Sometimes I wonder what would have happened if I'd ended up at Trammell Crow or somewhere else in New York—a place that I felt somehow not cut out for or fundamentally interested in. I likely would have left to pursue my own interests. But likely, just as I had enjoyed so many people in my undergraduate experience, I would have enjoyed working with whatever group of people I ended up with. The fact is that smart, dedicated people are almost always interesting. We can all fall into the trap of provincialism, so maybe Trammell or Goldman would have turned out well too, though in a completely different way. There's no way to ever know which fork in the road is the right one to take and where it would have led. Deep down, though, I knew instinctively that I was different from my peers who desperately wanted those jobs in those companies. As usual, I may not have been completely sure of what my next step would be, but by now I was starting to trust myself enough to believe that I would know when the right thing—for me—appeared.

# THE HYDROELECTRIC PROJECT

During my undergraduate years, between 1980 and 1984, I would drive down to Hartford, Connecticut, on weekends to visit Henry. He was an actual mechanical engineer now, working for Nome's father. Mr. Perry, as I called him, was also off-the-charts brilliant, and his engineering company, E. M. Perry (now Perry Technology), produced very specialized helical gears that were so high-tech and reliably precise that they were often used on NASA space shuttles. Henry had learned a lot from Mr. Perry all those years ago from the dining-room-blackboard symposia, and it seemed to be really paying off: He was developing a company that manufactured low-head hydroelectric turbines——the mechanical rotary device that converts water energy into electrical power—and the particular kind often used on the East Coast, where river-flow drops might be fifty to a hundred feet.

Having spent a lot of time in Europe throughout my childhood and young adulthood, particularly in the Alps and in Germany and Switzerland—where 16 percent of total electric generation comes from hydro—I, too, saw an opportunity in developing hydroelectric power in Colorado in an economical way. When it was clear that tax credits could be used by the skiwear company, I set up a company that was a subsidiary of Sport Obermeyer and spent my undergraduate summers driving through the most mountainous parts of Colorado in search of prospective hydroelectric sites. I soon realized that summer wasn't the right time for this kind of search—everything looked good then, after the snowmelt, when the rivers were roaring, so I narrowed the possibilities and revisited those sites in the fall and winter. If there was good flow at that time of year, then you'd have enough power output year-round.

This was shortly after the energy crisis during the Carter administration, when Congress had passed rules to increase the production of electricity to try to lower prices. There was a 10 percent investment tax credit and a 15 percent energy tax credit, incentives that helped spur investments in all kinds of alternative energy infrastructure projects. In addition, the Public Utilities Regulatory Policies Act acknowledged that while the distribution of electricity is a natural monopoly (you don't want to have ten different sets of power lines coming in or down each driveway), producing electricity could be deregulated, which increased competition. Requiring the utilities to buy power was part of that deregulation (the utility companies didn't like it) and they also had to wheel the power—transmit it—from one place to another. (What we were developing would wheel power from southwestern Colorado to the eastern slope.) A mini-boom of hydroelectric projects regulated by the Federal Energy Regulatory Commission (FERC) and other agencies was underway, and I was confident that I wanted to pursue my project if I could find a site that made economic sense.

Without going into all the details, which could fill a book of their own, these are the highlights of how my hydroelectric project developed: I purchased a company called Ptarmigan Resources & Energy, a shell company that had a preliminary permit to develop a site using the existing Vallecito Dam in southwestern Colorado near Durango. Their plan had run into the economic hurdle of not being profitable as a 2.5-megawatt site, which it had been conceived as and licensed for. I realized

I could use that company to amend the license and develop a project in a way that would be profitable: specifically, to nearly double the power output without doubling the cost of the project.

Henry, who had significant expertise in the field of hydraulics, came up with a solution to use the full head of the Vallecito Reservoir by pressurizing a nine-foot-diameter penstock—the large steel pipes that bring water from the reservoir to a turbine—from the dam to a yet-to-be-built powerhouse with enough turbine capacity to capture the full potential of that water pressure. The good news was that the dam, its spillway, and the outlet tunnel existed, and the water was being used to supply the Pine River Irrigation District for their agricultural needs. The not-so-good news was that everything else would need to be built: the penstock, the powerhouse, the turbines it would house, and all the engineering, computor monitoring, and mechanical parts fundamental to running a successful hydroelectric facility.

A project like this would require multiple key players to make it work: the southern Ute Indian tribe that held the senior water rights; the irrigation district; the electric company to wheel the power from the site to the transformer that would distribute it to the five thousand or so homes it could power; the engineering companies that would build the project; the company in Scotland that would make the custom turbines; FERC; the Bureau of Reclamation; and, of course, the bankers, whom I would have to convince to trust a kid like me to make it all happen.

Enter Monty Deckerd, who oversaw the energy division of the Bank of Minneapolis. Very few banks in the country were giving loans for a project of this size, but Monty ran one of them. I had worked incredibly hard on the financials, going over the calculations repeatedly until I thought I had them right. Still, when I flew out there and got dressed for my meeting, I was extremely nervous—and it didn't help that when I went to put on the suit I'd bought at Keezer's for my Goldman interview, it didn't fit—likely because I was no longer trying to make weight on the lightweight crew team the way I was when I'd bought it. It was now easily two sizes too small, and I could barely move my arms or zip the pants. Luckily, Monty didn't seem to notice or care. I presented my workup for the project, and, miraculously, he approved it. To this day, he says it was one of the most on-budget and detailed plans he's had the privilege to finance. Monty and his kids are clients of OWP today, and we have maintained a relationship all these years that I cherish. This was the first of many strong and respectful relationships I have made over the past thirty years of working on this project.

With the financing in place, I needed to buy the Scottish-made turbines because they had the longest lead time for production. I was pretty sure about the calculations for the power and the cost of materials: Between the turbines and generators, it would be a little over $2 million, though the actual hard costs for all the equipment would likely be somewhere around $4.5 million. I still needed to figure out who was going to supply everything else we needed, and I still didn't even have a license from FERC. By the time I'd graduated from business school, I had the tiger by the tail—"all" I had to do now was make it work. I knew that General Electric was building and installing hydro projects around the country, and that John Estes and Barry Post were two great guys who knew their stuff and were working in that division. They had built the hydroelectric facility at Ruedi Reservoir, down the road from Emma, where I'd grown up, and they would go on to start their own company, E Squared Power Systems Inc. I hired $E^2$ to do the electrical plan and design for the project; Brent Gardner to do the civil engineering work; and Hamilton Brothers, a civil construction company out of Utah, to start working on the penstock and mechanical engineering aspects.

As with most complex projects of this scope and scale, there are critical moments where decisions need to be made. One of those moments came when I had ordered the turbines but had not yet heard anything from FERC about whether they were even going to consider my application. FERC is a huge bureaucratic government organization with a reputation for working at their own pace, and we were not a priority; it could take years for them to get around to reviewing and signing off on my little project. But I didn't have years: I had to order the penstock, which was going to be another million dollars, if I wanted to move the project forward. Needless to say, I was stressed, so I called my dad for advice. "Wally," he said. "When you ordered the turbines, you jumped off the high-dive board. Now you have to hit the water going straight. There's no going back now." Although I would have liked more comforting advice, I knew that he believed in me and felt I could do it. And I must have, deep down, believed in myself too, because I had enough confidence to keep going.

It worked out in the end: FERC came through; the Bureau of Reclamation became a wonderful partner and resource, particularly Pat Schumacher and later Randy Green; and I've been thankful for the long relationship with the Pine River Irrigation District. Joe Brown was the dam keeper when we built the project, and he went on to run it for the next ten years; Christy, his daughter, was the office manager and plant operator until she retired in 2024. These are some of the finest people I have met in my life, and I consider them great friends to this day. In retrospect, my one regret is that I didn't get to know the leadership of the Utes better. I felt they were not adequately represented, and I hope that is rectified in the future. There are long-standing rivalries in the West that are finally being addressed such that all parties are being heard.

Looking back on the years I spent developing the Vallecito Dam project and Ptarmigan Resources actively after business school, from 1986 to 1989 until it got up and running, I sometimes wonder how I had the guts to do something as risky as that. From my current vantage point, of course, I can only think of all the ways the project could have been a disaster, but back then, it all seemed like a fun, exciting tightrope of a challenge. That's what being young is all about: You know you'll have plenty of time to correct mistakes down the road. Youth and time and not fully grasping all of what you don't know gives you the courage and the blissful ignorance to take risks, to follow a passion project through to completion even if you don't have all the answers when you start out. This project eventually led me back to Colorado, and its success would, in time, give me the confidence to jump off other high-dive boards, each time trying again to hit the water straight.

# IN THE AIR

I grew up around planes because my dad flew, though for him, flying was more of a convenience than a passion. Flying is an unforgiving venture, and you need to be wired for that sort of attention to detail, that level of commitment to following rules and regulations, the way I am. I had always wanted to learn to fly, but after I had graduated high school and was working in the summers repping skiwear for Sport Obermeyer, I finally had a reason to pursue getting my pilot's license. My territory was vast: Idaho and Montana, Wyoming and Utah. The distances in that part of the world are long, and driving took forever. Flying would allow me to connect with significantly more people in person than driving ever would. I took lessons in Aspen, and got my private pilot license within the year.

My first plane was a Cessna 182 that I rented during the time I was working on the hydro project, making hundreds of flights back and forth from Colorado Springs, where I lived at the time. After that, Sport agreed to buy a company plane: a Cessna 180 taildragger, N3484Y, which I still have to this day. It's a super-practical plane for rural areas where there aren't many airports. Taildraggers allow you to land on dirt and grass strips, or, in a pinch, in a farmer's field. The tail drops when you land while the propeller tips up so it won't hit the ground and cause an accident. Many of the planes you see in Alaska are taildraggers for this reason. I'd hired a renowned member of the Aspen flying community, Bob Fulton, to help me find a plane, and we settled on one in Minnesota. When Bob went out to pick it up, he flew through terrible weather, forcing him to land in Denver's old Stapleton International Airport around midnight, where he slept on a couch in the FBO (fixed base operation) before continuing on to Aspen in the morning. It was lucky the plane and Bob made it. He was a true pilot's pilot.

"There are old pilots and bold pilots but no old, bold pilots" is a saying in our world. Bob was a very bold pilot, and sadly he is no longer with us as a result. He taught me how to fly that airplane, which isn't easy because the tail wheel makes it challenging to control on takeoff and landing (later I did an IO-470 conversion to the engine from a carburetor system to a fuel-injection system, which added only 4 percent to the weight but 24 percent to the output). In the realm of C180s, it's a little rocket: At the Aspen airport, you're airborne before the commercial aircraft apron. Some friends of mine would laugh to hear me make that claim about the plane. Once, when I was flying with Bill Buddinger to Los Angeles, there was such a strong headwind that we thought we might actually be going backward. Bill is a great pilot, who mostly flies jets, so I doubt that he ever ventured to take another trip in a little Cessna, but for me, that plane is perfect. It's flying at its most basic, its most stripped down, its most pure and simple form. To me, flying that plane is as close to feeling like you're a bird as it's possible to feel.

One flight that exemplifies the beauty of this plane happened in May 2010. It was a glorious morning after a big late-season dump of snow the night before, and Helen and I jumped out of bed and drove to the airport. The sky was blue, the snow was sparkling, there was no wind: It was a perfect day to fly. We headed into the peaks around Aspen. Capitol Peak is a renowned fourteener (a mountain that stands over fourteen thousand feet) because to climb it, you have to traverse a knife-edge about eighteen inches wide to get to the summit. As we went by the knife-edge, Helen saw something completely unexpected. "Wally! There are footprints on the edge!" she said.

But there couldn't be. Who would be up there after a big snowstorm that early in the morning? It's five to six hours to the base from which you ascend Capitol Peak, so someone would have had to go the day before, in the snow, to be there now. But when we circled back, sure enough, Helen was right—there were footprints in the snow on the knife-edge. As we continued, three skiers launched into the big bowl right below the summit and made perfect S-turns all the way to the bottom. Mesmerizing to watch, it looked and felt like magic. As it turned out, one of the people who had made the footprints was our friend Christy Mahon, and that was the last of the fifty-four fourteeners she had ascended and skied. Only seven people had ever completed this remarkable feat, and she was the first woman to do so. Days later when we made the connection between the airplane she saw circling and our witnessing her descent, her reaction was so Christy: "I am so pissed! Why didn't you drop us a few beers?!"

I went on to get my instrument rating, which allowed me to fly in the clouds or at night using avionics. I partnered in those years in a P210, got my twin-engine certification, and bought a Cessna 414, N220RR. Eventually, looking for more speed, I got a TBM 700, N700WE. As my finances increased, so did my access to better capability and utility in the aircraft I owned; by the time I had the TBM, Obermeyer Wealth Partners had clients in nearly forty states, and I could fly to all of them. Most recently, I bought a Pilatus NG, which is the apex of my collection, and which brings me pure joy. Pilatus is a Swiss-made turboprop plane and represents all the beauty and integrity you would expect from a Swiss company. An engineering marvel that is very sexy (even my wife agrees), it has an enormous cargo door that allows you to load it up with friends and gear for whatever adventure you're taking; a range of two thousand nautical miles; and deicing capabilities—all of which means I can fly her in most weather conditions. N925ZG (*925* being the first three numbers of all the old Aspen phone numbers and *ZG* the letters on the traditional Aspen license plates) is my baby. There hasn't been a single time that I've gone to the airport when she's been out on the tarmac and I haven't felt a visceral thrill, and a deep sense of gratitude that I get to do something I love so much in such a beautiful aircraft.

In case I haven't made it clear enough already, I love absolutely everything about airplanes and flying. The physics of flight, the attention that must be paid to weather, the complexity of the mechanics, the specificity of running and maintenance, the flight planning, the importance of the checklist, and the camaraderie of the pilot community—it all speaks to me and resonates on some very deep level. The meticulousness required for all aspects of flying and aircraft maintenance suits my personality perfectly. When talking about airplane ownership, most people cite convenience and freedom and even the status of plane ownership, but for me, the idea that you're never done learning is what's most compelling. Every flight teaches me something new.

I've always prided myself on doing more than what is expected in terms of training and maintenance, so while the Federal Aviation Administration requires one training session a year on simulators, most years I have not only done that, I have also done flight training in the air with an instructor. I'm proud to say that I studied for and passed my Airline Transport Pilot rating, which would allow me to fly for any commercial airline, assuming I passed the appropriate check rides for the specific planes I would be captaining. This commercial pilot certification is not necessary for the kind of flying I do, but I will always go the extra mile to be as safe as possible. Education and training and retraining is a big part of that.

Mastering a machine, appreciating the art and preciseness of it, understanding the constant variability of it, and knowing I need to be ready for any eventuality delights me. It's why I keep a book to record my thoughts and to try after every flight to answer the question "What did I learn on this flight?" With each new experience, I try to understand what set of conditions led to it: Maybe it was a good night's sleep or being really well hydrated; maybe it was being so ahead of the planning that I felt especially well prepared. One of my favorite things to do when I'm preparing to fly a group of passengers is to get to the airport a good thirty to forty-five minutes early so that I have time to do a nice, thorough preflight, get the windows cleaned and oil checked, and make sure that everything is set and ready to go. That extra time alone to focus and prepare is immensely calming.

Like everything in life, it's not just the places you go but the people you meet along the way. I always look forward to going to the airport and seeing various members of the piloting community who have become such good friends: Jeff Yusum, Peter Hudder, Bruce and Janie, Bubba, Jerry—everyone enjoying tinkering away on Saturday or Sunday mornings, caring for their aircraft. I've built friendships over the years with all the hardworking line staff who fuel, park, handle luggage, and help maintain the planes, and I have total respect for the skill and responsibility they take moving multimillion-dollar planes in all weather conditions. It always feels great to get back from a trip and see Brian giving me a welcome-home smile.

Andrew Doremus is a skilled pilot, friend, and taskmaster of a teacher who taught me a great deal while training me on the C414. During the hours in the air, we had many laughs about our families and his tales of wonderful and awful clients he'd flown during his career as a private pilot. I'm not too shy to admit that I have a total pilot crush on Tyson Weihs, founder and CEO of ForeFlight, who transformed the flying industry from using paper charts that needed to be filed and updated in heavy binders to having all the latest charts available and accessible electronically on the iPad. Not only is he a great pilot, he understands the competitive advantage companies with an aviation component of their business have: how getting out to see clients and projects in the time-efficient way that flying enables makes a huge difference all around. And Bruce Gordon and Jane Pargiter, a couple in Aspen, turned their passion for flying and conservation into EcoFlight, a wonderful business that advocates for protecting wildlands and habitat by flying people so they can see from the air what is happening to the environment.

My flying partner, Micah, has the same love of aviation that I do—we both felt while growing up that there was nothing cooler than being a pilot. We also were both influenced by singer-songwriter and actor John Denver's passion for flying: In a sense, John, who was incredibly famous at the time as an icon of the music world and a poster child for the natural beauty and outdoor lifestyle of Colorado, was less a celebrity to us as just a great example of someone who loved flying as much as we did. I remember being up in the Aspen Tower when a flight controller handed me a pair of binoculars. "Here comes John," he said. "He's flying the plane. Let's see how his landing is."

Micah's dad loved John's music—"Rocky Mountain High" and "Starwood in Aspen"—and whenever he heard that John would be flying in, he would run out to the FBO in hopes of meeting him. That finally happened when Micah was about fourteen. He and his dad were at the FBO when John arrived. After the grown-ups had talked, John took young Micah out and showed him his plane. He put Micah in the pilot's seat, fastened the seat belt, and fired up the airplane. That's when Micah knew he wanted to become a pilot.

Flying has given me countless hours of happiness during family vacations and adventures with friends. But I think that if I scrolled through all of my memories of flights the way Helen scrolls through all of my phone photos, one flight would stand out from all the others: the time I flew to Dubois, Wyoming, in the Cessna 180 with Helen and my stepdaughters to watch the total solar eclipse in August of 2017. The little municipal airport, which was among those in the path of totality, was almost comically full of private aviators like us who had flown there to witness this once-in-a-lifetime event. As we sat in our chairs that morning with our glasses on, looking up at the sky as around us it got cold and windy, the light faded to the point that we wondered if the pilot of the helicopter hovering overhead would log that time as night flying. Darkness fell for almost two full minutes, and we were awed by the wonder of it all and by the deep gratitude of getting to experience a moment of such spectacular and unparalleled beauty together. When it was over and the light returned, I did something you can only do when you know the territory well: I knew there were no telephone or electric wires on our route, so we flew fast and very low, passing over herds of wild horses and antelope that ran in front of us in the open grasslands between the Wind River Range and the Elk Mountains toward home. It was truly an *Out of Africa* moment. We were all whooping with delight. I can't think of anything that encapsulates the magic and joy of flying more than that afternoon.

Lift

It's always a good day to fly!

The other woman

My happy place

Sharing my passion

Catherine's Christmas gift to me

A favorite pastime, capturing bucolic Aspen days

Serene Aspen days

The joy of becoming a grandparent

Family fun

Natalie, Matt, William, Emma, and Eleanor

The warmth of family

Treasured moments

Best of friends: lunch after a long hike in the Swiss Alps

My love for Brown Swiss cows

Mountain living

Beach bliss

We made it! Kilimanjaro 2019

A birthday gift for my in-laws, Jim and Carol Swiggett

Flying together, our happy place

Klaus and EJ's engagement, Sun Valley

Boxes of Swiss sweaters arrive for sale, Aspen

Arrival of Nome, Aspen

Nome and her mom, Mrs. Perry

Me and Michael, *freche Buben*, Emma

Me with Grandma Mina, Grandpa Fritz, and Cousin Fritz, Oberstaufen

Grandpa Fritz, leading the parade

Aunt Cilly's famous meals

My cherished Aunt Cilly

With my beloved cousin Michael and his wife, Jenny

Michael and Jenny visiting us in Tübingen

My lovely milk cow Silky Milky

Big sellers: mirrored sunglasses and striped ski sweaters

Ad for the ski brakes we invented during my ski patrol days

My love for skiing

End-of-season fun during my ski patrol days

Early photo of Klaus in Germany

Dr. Patterson and grandkids

Me with Tom Patterson, Crestone Needle

Me, Tom, and Bill Patterson

Crew team

Crew team at work

Crew team 25th reunion

Crew team reunion bike trip, seated in our positions, Moab

Ptarmigan hydroelectric plant

Checking the dam at Vallecito

Turbines in the hydroelectric plant

Sharing my passion for hydro with Catherine

Mini me: me and William

Best day of flying: watching the eclipse and flying through
the Wind River Range, Wyoming

Sharing my love of sport: Dad, Klaus Jr., and me

My "little" brother, Klausie

Suzan the equestrian

Suzan the artist

Suzan at her art show with my niece Laura

At home in Oberstaufen

Henry the engineer

Starting the business and early advertising

Wally Obermeyer

Focused investment
strategies for those who
appreciate planning

Heritage Trust &
Asset Management, Inc.

616 E. Hyman, Suite 102
Aspen, CO 81611
(303) 925-8747

Wally Obermeyer

"Let's talk."

Heritage Trust &
Asset Management, Inc.

616 E. Hyman, Suite 102
Aspen, CO 81611
(303) 925-8747

Management team, 2023

The broader team at Obermeyer Wealth Partners
attending a client event in Vail in 2025

Me with my hero, Warren Buffett

A big moment, getting an award from Steve Forbes

Berkshire Hathaway annual meeting with Katie

Part of the OWP team getting ready to hear Warren and Charlie's wisdom at the 2022 Berkshire Hathaway Annual Shareholder Meeting in Omaha

My partner Ali

Ali providing market analysis on one of her regular appearances
on CNBC's *Closing Bell* program

Ali speaking on firm leadership at the SHOOK *Forbes*
Top Women Advisor Summit in 2024

Make new friends but keep the old . . . my cherished
Willys Jeep and Cessna 180

# THE SPORT OBERMEYER
# SUPPLY CHAIN METHOD

There was a time when most people at a ski resort in America were wearing Obermeyer turtlenecks and Obermeyer-designed jackets. I can remember skiing with Helen a few years ago as ski school in Snowmass was starting, when she turned to me and said, "This is like an advertisement for Obermeyer!" And it was. My father had taken his love for skiing and turned it into a successful skiwear business whose signature was not just well-made clothing and gear but an exuberant love for the sport. My father had infused joy and optimism into every aspect of the company.

That day on the slopes, almost every child we saw was wearing Obermeyer. We have Nome to thank for this aspect of the business—she had a particular knack for creating kids' ski clothes that appealed to both kids and parents. Like all Obermeyer gear, it was good-looking, of course, but more important was that it did what my dad wanted it to do: It kept you warm, it was practical, and it was made for skiers. No matter how much skiing has become an elite sport with many manufacturers capitalizing on their wealthy clientele by providing high-end ski apparel at sometimes exorbitant prices, my dad never wanted to go that route. He never sacrificed utility for style; he always wanted to provide access to anyone interested in skiing. The materials are the best, and the designs make perfect sense— pockets are where you need them to be, the pants give you room to move through those moguls, and you're never going to get a blast of snow up your pant leg or down your back on even the biggest powder days.

The kids' line developed I-Grow, which is now an industry standard. I-Grow allows you to remove stitching so the pant legs and arms of the clothes can grow along with a child. After business school when I worked for the skiwear company for a time, I occasionally would suggest ways to maximize profitability: Maybe the kids' line should last for fewer than four years; maybe we should get parents to buy new ski clothes for their kids every year instead. But my dad always took great offense at those sorts of ideas. "Wally! *Sie können nur ein steak pro nacht essen*," he would admonish me. *You can only eat one steak a night.* This was his way of saying that his motivation was not to make more money. His motivation was to make a quality product that people trusted and could rely on. That core business belief is connected to another core belief and one of his constant refrains: "Your reputation is your working capital. You can build it over a lifetime and lose it in an instant." These simple and sound philosophies, and many others, are at the heart of my own business practices too. They're the foundation on which everything I've built rests and another one of the many gifts my dad gave me.

Thomas Wolfe may have said you can't go home again, but that's exactly what I did in 1989: I returned to Aspen and came back to work for Sport Obermeyer. It was after business school and after working on the hydroelectric project from San Francisco, where I'd moved with my first wife, Susan—we had met at HBS, and she'd gotten a job there with an HMO. I knew at the time that Northern California would be temporary and that I would eventually head back to Colorado, both because the hydro project was based outside of Durango and because on some level I always knew I'd return to help in the family business; it seemed like the most natural route to take. I'd learned things, I'd seen things—I would share that knowledge and make some good and necessary changes to help the business and the team grow. What could possibly go wrong?

By 1992, in advance of figuring out production for the 1993–1994 season, I had become very interested in how we made decisions about production quantities for each of our clothing items. At the time, we were forecasting very accurately for about half of the styles we sold: Extrapolating from about 10 percent of the orders received from dealers, we would regularly come within a 5 to 10 percent error range. Given how many units we had within every style and all the choices for all the different items—different colors and sizes for five segmentations based on gender and age (men, women, boys, girls, and preschoolers) and different customer types within those gender lines depending on the type of skier they were—we were figuring things out with amazing accuracy. Still, I knew that we had to improve on our predictions to minimize both the overproduction of items that our retail partners wouldn't end up ordering and shortages of items that had become unexpectedly popular. My question was, with those few orders in, which half did we forecast accurately and why?

I went back to HBS and asked one of my professors if he knew who I might reach out to for help with this dilemma. When he told me that Jan Hammond was working on these very issues related to supply chain management, I was delighted; this was the very same Jan who had been my professor for the very first class I took at HBS. When I contacted her, she was also delighted, not just because we had always shared a bond from that first encounter but also because she was so deeply interested and immersed in these very vexing and fascinating opportunities for forecasting better outcomes. Once we'd reconnected, she introduced me to a colleague of hers at Wharton, Marshall Fisher, with whom she had worked extensively and who had a very bright graduate student working with him, Ananth Raman (he would end up joining the HBS faculty and is still teaching there today). Together, the four of us formed the team for our supply chain project. Our goal was to integrate and improve on business-school-type forecasting methods for supply chain management to optimize sales and production by minimizing waste and creating a stable supply chain.

One thing we found was that we could improve our forecasting by keeping track of our buying committee's previous forecast accuracy. We had always forecasted as a group, where the most vocal and overconfident people would influence everybody else. It seemed to me that was a problem. We found that when the merchandisers presented to the buying committee, forecasting improved when people voted individually and privately, instead of publicly, the way we had before. What we learned was that if everybody agreed that a certain style was a dog, it was a dog; if everybody loved a certain style, it was a winner. There was a very low variance, a low standard deviation in the forecast: The forecast error was low, making it possible to go ahead and get the production started early for those styles. We could focus on the other styles later, after we had more information from more orders coming in.

Our work focused on improving the accuracy of our forecasting, which enabled us to be very efficient in determining ahead of time how we would go about manufacturing, since we could forecast the styles that were most likely to be the most popular and would require the biggest runs and get them under production. Certain factories required bigger runs, while smaller runs or more specialty items could be manufactured in other places. This also helped us decide on where we would manufacture based on labor and materials-sourcing issues. We also had to take into account the increasing competition from other sportswear companies: There were products we needed to make because consumers wanted them, but they were products that consumers were very price sensitive to since there wasn't much difference between the companies that made those products. In those cases, we needed to work with factories that were producing lower-priced items at a higher volume and had to make operational changes to improve supply chain cost and timing issues.

When our research and recommendations were completed, we published our findings in *The Harvard Business Review* in October 1994. The study ended up on the front page of some of the top supply chain management magazines in the country and eventually became an HBS case study that is still taught today both at Harvard and Stanford. Executives from top companies, including Dell and Siemens in Germany, among many others, came to Aspen to study and learn about the Obermeyer Supply Chain Method.*

* The case study can be read at https://onlinelibrary.wiley.com/doi/abs/10.1111/j.1937-5956.1997.tb00427.x

# THE GO-AROUND

A go-around is a flight maneuver that diverts from a planned and anticipated landing. Sometimes called a missed approach, it's usually done when there are unsafe ground conditions, like strong winds, or debris on the runway, or too many planes trying to come in. Timing and safety is everything, and a pilot knows when it's better, even on a final approach, to change course and return to the air.

My experience being back at Sport during that period was making me wonder if I should try to land again—somewhere else. While my father had reluctantly agreed to implement the changes I'd recommended, he was suspicious of academics and disliked prioritizing systems over instinct. He also didn't like the attention I was getting in the press for our innovations in supply chain management. When the companies who were interested in what we were doing sent representatives to tour our facility, he grumbled and did his best to win them over with his charismatic personality. For two or three years, we butted heads. While inventory and ordering did improve, he was never completely comfortable with the concepts I'd introduced. Our system wasn't perfect, but we did begin to match production with end-product demand more effectively. Still, the cost of missing a sale was greater than the cost of overproduction, so sometimes we weren't cautious enough with our numbers and ended up with excess inventory. That was something tangible my dad could point to, and it galled him. Numbers are only one part of running a business, and, in the end, while I was fascinated with spreadsheets and analytics, my dad was more interested in running the business as he always had—through relationships and following his gut sense for what trends would motivate people to buy. I was able to keep my supply chain management concept in place for about two or three years, but there was definitely tension in the office.

Another of our biggest points of contention centered on competition in the marketplace. During these years, there was a huge amount of consolidation among retailers and the expansion of big-box stores like REI and Sports Authority, and they were chipping away at our margins and our market share. In that time span, we had gone from selling to about twenty-four hundred stores to six hundred stores—a huge shift in a fifteen-year period that put a lot of stress on all the suppliers in the business. It also resulted in companies like REI being able to make basic items like vests and jackets more cheaply than Sport Obermeyer could, while benefiting from greater margins because they had no middleman. My dad felt utterly loyal to the ski retailers he'd always considered to be true partners, and continued to hold out, ensuring they would be the biggest purveyors of our product. Online retail was another trend gaining momentum at that time, but, similarly, Dad would not hear about selling Obermeyer products that way. Both Klausie and I tried to convince him otherwise, but he would not do it.

My father and I disagreed in other ways too, especially when it came to how we treated and showed appreciation to our hardworking team. I believe very strongly in empowering people to make their own decisions and feel good about their input and the outcome, and I felt that education and training in the form of professional development, including business school–type seminars, was appropriate and helpful to them and to us. To put it mildly, my dad did not like this sort of thing at all, and his unwillingness to spend company money on seminars and conferences put us at a difficult impasse: When it came to what I considered very important aspects of team-building, my father simply did not share my views. But I continued to hold out hope that we would eventually be able to come to some kind of workable compromise on our core beliefs.

I'd been at Sport Obermeyer after business school for almost eight years by then, and the impasse had only become more pronounced and undeniable during that time. There were a number of fundamental differences in how we envisioned the company moving forward and how we thought the team should function, and by that point I knew we would never square them. I was a few years shy of forty, well into my second marriage, and finally realizing that my father was simply not someone who wanted a partner. He was a maverick—creative, spontaneous, full of light and energy—and any attempts to change or control those instincts and impulses were, and always would be, met with resistance. I was becoming increasingly clear about our differences, and increasingly comfortable with those differences. I knew I was ready for change.

My dad has always said that the greatest freedom in life is that we have the choice of how we view things. And there was a switch that turned on for me where I finally realized that there was a solution to this problem—and that solution was an opportunity. I knew that if he were ever to retire, he might lose his zest for life, which meant that it was incumbent on me to go do something that I wanted to do. And what I wanted to do was create something on my own and build a team and a business that operated in ways that made sense to me and made me happy. That switch in mentality—of clearly seeing that there were two ways of thinking about the business and that ours did not overlap—made it possible for me to leave. When I'd made up my mind, I tried to communicate my thoughts and feelings to Nome and my dad, assuring them that I loved them and that this would be a positive move for all of us. I wrote them a very heartfelt note, one that I came across recently, which said something like, "There are many ways to be an effective coach, and it's not that one way is right and the other is wrong, but our ways are very different. I love you, and I'm moving forward." While I had hoped they would accept my decision with grace and understanding and wish me well, there were hard feelings for a few years. Thankfully, those eventually passed, and we all are better for knowing that in the end, taking separate paths was the right way for all of us to go.

# SAFE LANDING

It's one thing to decide on and execute a go-around; it's another thing to find a good alternative place to land to start a new and positive future. While I'd had some business successes at Sport and with the hydroelectric project that I was proud of, the person who gave me an entrée into the investment business where the next phase of my life would start and eventually flourish was Dr. Patterson, whom I spoke about earlier. He was an outstanding investor, and he introduced me to value investing, and to Warren Buffett, and to so many other thinkers who would become my most trusted influences. Dr. Patterson was the opposite of the Texas expression I'd grown up hearing, "Big hat, no cattle." He had no hat, and he had a ton of cattle. He simply worked hard and always did the right thing, no matter what situation he was in. To this day, I have a huge amount of respect and a deep well of gratitude for him.

Dr. Patterson was on the board of an independent trust company, Heritage Trust and Asset Management Inc, which was doing reasonably well in Grand Junction, and he was thinking about the possibility of opening an office in Aspen. I mentioned that I was considering leaving Sport Obermeyer, and Dr. Patterson offered to connect me to Heritage. When the president of Heritage and I eventually spoke, we liked each other well enough, but he made it clear during our negotiations that the pay would not be overly generous. That was cause for concern. Without really thinking, I blurted, "Well, if I'm ever unhappy in that regard, I'll just start my own company." My impulsive comment would cost me a noncompete clause in my contract, but in the end, it would be worth it because while my noncompete clause stipulated that I would agree not to compete against Heritage Trust, I also negotiated the right of first refusal should their Aspen branch ever be sold.

My go-around now complete, I opened a one-room office for Heritage on Hyman Avenue in Aspen in 1994. Doing so was either a brave leap of faith or an incredibly stupid one—thinking that I could start something new, from scratch, in a field I knew almost nothing about, in my forties, was due to either courage or hubris. I'll admit that in those early months and years I vacillated between both conclusions. Not surprisingly, those first few years were a struggle: The investment business has always been a relationship business, built on connections and word of mouth—it was hard to keep the faith during those lean times with very little revenue coming in, and there were more than a few long nights when I would come home for dinner, put the boys to bed, and then go back to the office, blast Fleetwood Mac, and work until two or three o'clock in the morning. Somehow, knowing that cultivating relationships would be the key to my survival and to the possibility of any future success, I kept my eyes on that prize, making calls to prospective clients I'd heard about through my existing relationships in Aspen, or who'd heard about me, and signing enough of them to gain some traction. That's not to say those calls were easy to make—I can remember one particularly stinging reply that began with the announcement that there was no way he was going to let a ski-parka salesman invest his money and ended with a dial tone when he hung up on me. I know it sounds like a cliché, but those moments almost always made me more determined to keep at it.

In time, though, we began to grow, and in 1997 there was an important pivot point: the announcement that Heritage Bank and Trust was being sold to Norwest Bank. It was this event that triggered my transition from being an employee of the bank to being the sole proprietor of an investment advisory firm when I bought out the Aspen assets from the bank and created Obermeyer Asset Management. After serving as regional vice president of Heritage Trust and Asset Management from 1994 to 1997, I was now the head of my own firm. When I bought out my portion of Heritage, there was about $60 million of assets under management at that time. What I gained, in addition to those business assets, was the reputational confidence that came when I called our customers and said, "Well, I have good news and bad news. The bad news is Heritage is being bought by Norwest, which has a branch in Aspen. The good news is I'm purchasing the Aspen assets and we can continue working together."

Back then, our minimums were one hundred thousand dollars, and I grandfathered everyone who had been a client at Heritage whether they met our new minimums or not. I always respected and took care of those who believed in me in the early days, and making sure customers felt that they were being thoughtfully taken care of is something we've maintained and continue to prioritize to this day. Many of those original customers are still customers at Obermeyer Wealth Partners, and at this point, they're also multigenerational customers. They love us for our level of personal service and commitment to protecting and growing their money, and we love them for their loyalty and trust. Relationships like these really do go both ways.

Takeoff is the phase of flight in which an aircraft goes through a transition from moving along the ground (taxiing) to flying in the air, and whenever I think about that elevation from bank employee to heading my own firm, I know that it was Dr. Patterson who gave me that crucial lift. He would continue to help me think things through after I bought out Heritage and started Obermeyer Asset Management, and I never stopped feeling incredibly lucky to have such a positive and benevolent mentor, someone who believed in me and my abilities to start over in a whole new field when I didn't yet believe in myself in those ways. He made it possible for me to change course in midlife, start again, and find work that has felt like a calling ever since. That time and those challenges weren't for the fainthearted, and I'll admit to having more than a few sleepless nights wondering if I'd made the right decision, but his support made all the difference in my ability to persist and thrive. He was, in Bette Midler's words, "the wind beneath my wings."

# STARTING OVER:
# FROM HERITAGE TO OWP

Aspen is basically a small town—a small town with a lot of global reach—and when Obermeyer Asset Management first started in early 1998, about 90 percent of our business came through word of mouth. We placed some small ads in the paper and sponsored a few events in town to get our name out there, but most of our leads came from people who had attended a dinner party, conference, or business meeting and heard about us when the conversation turned to investments.

And by "us" I mean Chris Goodendorf, Roger Hennefeld, and me (Brad Zanin, who'd been helping me transition from Heritage to my own investment advisory firm, and I were officially the first two employees of OAM in early 1998). After a few people came and went, Chris joined us in June, primarily as a front desk person and receptionist. Shortly after that, Roger came on board as a trader. We three started out in that same little office on Hyman Avenue in downtown Aspen, in what was once a Christmas store in an old building with old wood floors that creaked, with about $60 million of assets from fifty or so clients; I could never have imagined then that we would be where we are now: at $2.5 billion, a fortyfold change in revenue, in just under thirty years.

As much as there was ever a typical day back then, one might have gone something like this: We'd get a daily download from Charles Schwab, our custodian. Chris, who had previously worked at what was then the Bank of Aspen and as a book-keeper at the Worldwide Ski Corporation, would take care of the mechanics of making sure all that information got converted into our system. That way, we could check on the accounts and make sure our clients had the liquidity they needed and that their trades and transfers had gone through. After that, I had client meetings. Following each one, I would dictate a letter to Chris with follow-up items to type up, and we would get it in the mail that same day. Between the two of us, we would make sure that all the follow-up action items in those letters were taken care of. After lunch, which Chris would usually pick up, she and I would go through the mail and whatever was on my desk, giving her on some days a huge stack of paper to be filed or otherwise handled. Times were so lean then—we were living off my line of credit to fund the company—that when we deducted the client fees from their accounts, she would immediately write a check and go to the bank to deposit it into the company account. Soon, Chris started opening new client accounts too, and I remember, in fact, helping her open her very first one. Both of us sat together at my desk as I walked her through the Schwab Link program. We were that small; we all did everything.

Around that time, in the fall, Roger joined us. A New Yorker by birth and personality, he had an MBA from the University of Colorado and had started his career in finance at Merrill Lynch in New York in the 1980s. When he realized that what he wanted most was to return to Colorado—he loved skiing on Aspen Mountain and hiking and biking in the Roaring Fork Valley—our mutual friend, Brad Zanin, connected us. In typical Roger fashion, he somehow managed to sidestep a formal interview with me, driving over to Aspen after a conference in Denver to meet spontaneously instead. Roger likes to say that he took a crumpled-up résumé from his back pocket and handed it to me, which I think I recall. But whether he did or not, I knew from our initial meeting that he was someone I should pay attention to. Roger had worked as an investment advisor with both back office and financial management experience, and not only was he a brilliant trader, but his knowledge of Axys, a portfolio management system that we were using at the time, as well as his programming skills for statements and billing and with spreadsheets, would soon become legendary in our office. Hiring Roger may have been a leap of faith at the time, but I don't know how we would have gotten off the ground and grown over all these years without him.

My evolution as a business owner, boss, and employer felt relatively smooth. Still, I've heard through the grapevine that it took me a bit of time to learn how to delegate—I'm very detail oriented and while I'm tolerant of mistakes, I've always believed that there's a lesson in every error, something important to be learned. Chris says that in her twenty-seven years with us, she's only heard me raise my voice twice. I hope that's true, but what I'm sure *is* true is that I'm not one of those people who flies off the handle and loses my temper when things go wrong; instead, I tend to remain calm and focus almost entirely on correcting the mistake and understanding why it happened and how to prevent it from happening again. My admonitions to myself in the early days around changing procedures to ensure the same mistake is not made again have turned into a company-wide policy in which errors become a company-wide training opportunity. There is no shame, no names mentioned, just the acknowledgment that something went awry and that processes need to be put in place to ensure that whatever happened does not happen again.

I would like to believe that this creates a positive culture of teamwork, learning how to fix problems together, rather than one of fear, in which people either try to hide their mistakes or blame others for them—a space where people feel able to take responsibility for their actions because they know they have a supportive team behind them.

The correction process always starts with a memo to me about exactly what happened, drafted by all the members of the team involved in that particular area of the business, so that I know what went wrong, why, and how we can fix the immediate situation. It also outlines any corrective measures to our processes and procedures. Chris jokes that the dreaded memo-writing process is my version of making someone write a lesson on a blackboard a hundred times—"I will not trade without preclearance," for instance—but nothing is more important than making things right and learning from our mistakes. Hence the memo method. I admit that it was challenging for me to let go of certain things. While I never stopped keeping a watchful eye on the business, I eventually began to adopt the Warren Buffett adage that I've already mentioned earlier in this book—that one about how a rising tide floats all boats—because in my continued evolution in the role of firm leader, I eventually realized that if I could let everyone do what they were great at and what we'd hired them for, if I let us all play to our strengths, we'd be better off as individuals and as a team.

My love of Buffett quotes and Klaus quips, which were born out of my father's optimism, made their way into my new company and some of my management decisions. Roger likes to remind me that for the first ten years of the firm, one of my "Klausisms" was deciding to sign everything with a smiley face next to my name. At that time, we would send out about 120 quarterly reports that Roger would generate and Chris would put together—which meant I would hand-sign every note that went out with them. Along with every signature, I would add a special little extra message—"I hope you're well"; "I hope you enjoyed your recent trip"—and then, of course, I'd draw a smiley face—☺ *Wally*. Needless to say, this little arts-and-crafts project took hours, and as the business grew, Roger tried to impress upon me that adding smiley faces by hand to client letters and mailings wasn't exactly the most efficient use of my time. After a brief negotiation, he agreed that I would be allowed to draw them on a very small number of letters for select clients. Eventually, he pushed me to lose them altogether—while it was a homey touch, he felt I didn't need to spend six hours every quarter drawing smiley faces. I'll admit that I was pretty heartbroken about it, but I'm not sure anyone else was, save for a few die-hard smiley-face lovers who called in to say they missed them. For those clients, I was still allowed to add my signature smiley faces to their letters until we phased them out. There was a funny incident, however, with the president of Alpine Bank. I also signed my checks with Alpine and put the smiley face in the memo section. One day during the phase-out period of the smiley faces, I wrote a sizable check for something related to the airplane—but with no smiley face. Chris received a call from Alpine Bank saying they thought someone was attempting to write a fraudulent check on my account. When she assured them that it was legitimate and asked why they thought otherwise, they told her: no smiley face ☺.

Those early days were a lot of fun, and Chris and I always had a special connection when it came to our humor. Our first big laugh came when I was on the phone giving the credit card company my billing information—whenever we needed to pay for something back then, we had to put the charge on my card—and when I was asked to spell my name and our office address, I answered: "616 East Hyman Avenue. Like the body part."

Chris, who was sitting right next to me—the office was so small that we did almost everything in close proximity—looked at me in a way that other people have looked at me throughout my life, in a way I now recognize as the look of astonishment at my complete and utter cluelessness.

"*Like the body part?*" she said once I was off the phone.

I nodded, and then, in my continued cluelessness, I turned to the only other person in the room for help. "Hey, Roger," I said, "where's your hymen?" When he informed me that he didn't have a hymen, and neither did I, Chris could no longer contain her laughter or the need to give me a much-needed lesson in female anatomy.

"Oh," I said, absorbing my new knowledge, which, of course, shouldn't have been new at all.

"Well, what did you think it was?" she asked.

"I thought a hymen was one of those organs near the pancreas."

I believe at that point she called me a bonehead, which was thoroughly deserved. Chris has always told me that she's the only woman who outlived all of my marriages combined, and I've always told her that she's the only person who knows about all my proverbial skeletons in the closet. Maybe that's why I've let her call me Spanky—her preferred nickname for me—all these years.

As we started adding people to our small team, including Ali Flynn Phillips in 2005, whom I'll talk more about in the next chapter, we broke through walls to adjoining offices twice to expand our space. But eventually we reached a point where we needed substantially more space. Our need for space and our family's development of Obermeyer Place dovetailed, and a year or so after it was completed, in around 2010, we moved our offices there, and that's where we've been ever since. It was a huge office with four people for many years. Now it's a small office for nine people. But our growth in Aspen was only the beginning: Just shy of ten years after starting OAM, when we had grown to seven or eight employees, were managing $550 to $600 million of assets, and were profitable, John on our team came to me and said that he had a friend in Denver who knew the market and could help us start and grow there. I was all for it. Acquiring our core presence in Denver in 2008 started small—a single room in an office building—but eventually it grew in clients and assets. About five years later, George Wood of Wood Investment Counsel in Denver and I started talking about a merger. I'd known him a bit through the business and from seeing him at conferences and other meetings, and I'd always felt that eventually we might do something together since we shared core values around long-term investment philosophy, serving families, and dedication to client service. As George got a little older and started thinking about retirement, we began to seriously discuss joining forces. In 2014 we merged to become Obermeyer Wood Investment Counsel.

Not everyone thought the merger was a great idea, mainly because bringing two firms together requires a great deal of work that goes beyond logistics. Two distinct cultures need to find common ground and processes, just as people with children who get remarried try to blend two families into one—it's never a certainty that combining forces will work. At first, we still felt like separate companies, because there were Wood clients and Obermeyer clients. They had their own custodian, and we had ours; they had their own billing, and we had ours. We felt much more like two entities sharing the same space than a single fully integrated company. Once we started getting new clients, though, clients were no longer a Wood client or an Obermeyer client; they were now an Obermeyer Wood client. Then we adopted new systems, which helped truly merge everything into one company that *feels* like one company, with about sixteen people in the Denver office, about ten in the Aspen office, and three in the Vail office, which is just getting started (the product of a merger with Adam Savin's Booth Creek Capital in early 2024). Booth Creek Capital was an Investment Manager that ran both US and European equity dividend strategies for family offices and ultra-high-net-worth individuals. With the merger we brought in investment expertise, family office experience, and an established local presence in a key strategic market. Ali and I would mostly go back and forth between Aspen and Denver, but there's fluidity among all our team members. Those based in Denver often want to come to Aspen for a long weekend of skiing, so they'll work in the Aspen office on a Friday and spend the rest of the weekend on the slopes, and Aspenites often hanker for a few days in the city. To bring everyone together and strengthen our connective ties, we hold yearly team retreats, off-site, just for team members. They are usually in the Vail area because it's equidistant from both main offices.

When I walk into one of our offices, I always take a moment and run through the names of all the people I'm likely to see. It delights me that so many new people are working with us. Diane Wallach, a dear friend who brought me onto the board at the Gates Family Foundation, has said, "Wally, the young always catch the old." One could take that as a negative, but the energy in our offices and the progress being made by this new generation gives me the same feeling I have when I'm accelerating down the runway and liftoff happens. It is forward momentum without friction, soaring rather than grinding. I am observing from above, delighted by the view.

# CREATING A TEAM THAT SWINGS

*The Boys in the Boat,* a number-one *New York Times* bestseller and later a film by the same name, tells the true story of the US men's rowing team from the University of Washington, who were the unlikely victors at the 1936 Berlin Olympics. Not only does the book provide an inspiring and epic example of fighting with grit and determination against the rise of fascism, but it also describes, in the words of the team's coach, what happens when people work together at the highest level of unity and synchronicity of movement and purpose:

> There is a thing that sometimes happens in rowing that is hard to achieve and hard to define. Many crews, even winning crews, never really find it. . . . It's called "swing." It only happens when all eight oarsmen are rowing in such perfect unison that no single action by any one is out of synch with those of all the others. . . . Only then will the boat continue to run, unchecked, fluidly and gracefully between pulls of the oars. Only then will it feel as if the boat is a part of each of them, moving as if on its own. Only then does pain entirely give way to exultation. Rowing then becomes a kind of perfect language. Poetry, that's what a good swing feels like.[*]

Poetry is what a good swing feels like with a great work team too. Maybe rowing crew all those years ago and experiencing

[*] Daniel James Brown, *The Boys in the Boat: Nine Americans and Their Epic Quest for Gold at the 1936 Berlin Olympics* (Penguin, 2013), 161.

swing myself firsthand gave me this deep and abiding love of true teamwork, whether it was at Harvard on the Charles River or anywhere else we raced, or with my colleagues at Sport Obermeyer, or beyond.

When I started OWP from Heritage, I wanted to create a team with swing. Reaching a perfect state of flow between our firm and our clients, understanding their needs and providing advice, guidance, reassurance when they need it most—supporting our team members in all the most important ways to allow them to flourish and thrive too—was my ultimate and ideal goal. Some years ago, when I was counseling a client on how to buy a piece of real estate—her dream home—she told me at the end of our call that since her dad had passed away fifteen years earlier, she'd turned to me as the go-to person for the kind of advice and counseling she wished she had from her dad and felt she still needed. Nothing exemplifies swing for me more than that. I love what I do, and I've loved getting up every day and going to work—to be part of a team that serves our wonderful clients, all of whom, in turn, inspire me.

Choosing people with complementary traits yet different personalities and backgrounds and appreciating each person for their individuality and what they bring to the group helps build a team with swing. There is no limit to what a team like that can accomplish. One of the biggest gifts Dad and Nome gave each of us kids was to support our strengths and not force us to live lives that went against our true natures. None of us followed a straight or traditional line to our eventual life's work, but we all ended up doing things that completely suited our personalities. I'm certain that has everything to do with how we were raised. Henry pursued engineering in all forms, as was his calling; Suzan followed her love of horses and art and was a wonderful caretaker to EJ in her later years, which led her to develop a keen interest in medical attributes of body work and massage. And while I felt a compulsion to join the family business at first, I eventually decided that what I wanted most was to start something of my own.

Klausie, the most like our father, was the least like me. He is a 100 percent physical person, happiest when jumping off a cliff in a hang glider, leaping over a small atoll in Fiji on his kite board, surfing with his blue heeler on the bow of his board in Malibu, or blasting through snow drifts in his snowmobile up near Ashcroft. He loves to spend what he earns and always has a new and exciting project or is off on a new adventure. He tends to soar, where I can be accused of plodding. While he was not the best student and didn't thrive in high school and never went to college, Nome understood that he processed life and learned visually and instinctively. She and my father helped him find a way of existing in the world that optimized his positive traits. Through the mentorship of John Wilcox, an extraordinary Emmy Award–winning filmmaker and television producer based in Aspen, Klausie built a successful career in film and advertising, cofounding Aéro Film, which was housed in a hangar next to Harrison Ford's at the Santa Monica Airport. The airport and Klausie's business have since closed, but Aéro, as its name suggested, specialized in aerial photography and developed several innovations in that field for steadying cameras and shooting out of helicopters and planes. It was the perfect job for someone whose drive in life is completely intuitive and action oriented.

Hiring is a mystery when building a team—especially when you aspire, as I do, to hire for life, to find people who will evolve and grow and help the team do the same. I have taken the lessons of my parents and looked for people who seem to have found a way to follow their own paths to our door. You can pretty quickly suss out the candidates whose résumés were cultivated by someone other than themselves, and although many of those people are smart and talented, rarely do you get the kind of passion I am after in hiring.

You can only see the tip of an iceberg when you meet someone, and you have to take a chance on what lies beneath the surface. One thing I always take into account is how a person has come to me—the often nontraditional route that brought them to where we've crossed paths, which seems like a kind of fate to me, a slightly magical synchronicity that has made a needle-in-a-haystack sort of match possible. I felt this way when I hired Ali in 2005 to work directly with clients, and it turned out to be one of the best decisions of my career—and hers too, I hope. She'd already had an impressive traditional career in finance, which included working in investment banking in Chicago, London, and Manhattan for Salomon Brothers and then Goldman Sachs, where she was vice president and worked with Lloyd Blankfein's staff. But it was her nontraditional route to Aspen and to the Obermeyer offices that piqued my interest: She and her husband Dave had left their successful careers in New York behind in search of something new, embarking on a three-month tour of the Rocky Mountains to try to figure out what they wanted to do next and where they wanted to live. When they got to Aspen, they felt a pull and decided to rent a place to give it a try for a year. How brave and gutsy and interesting a series of choices was that?

Our first meeting was more of an informational conversation than an interview—the Aspen-based father of a college classmate of Ali's had connected us at a time when we weren't hiring. But later, when she called again, I told her to come back in, because by that point we were looking for someone to help grow the firm. Even though Ali had never worked with individual clients on the wealth management side of the business, I sensed from how down-to-earth she was and how easily we were able to communicate and connect meaningfully that she was the right person at the right time to join us. It seemed that her geographical and emotional journey west had made her realize that what she loved most about working in finance was the relationships with the companies and people she'd worked with—and that what she wanted to lean into moving forward was working with individuals and families on the wealth management side. While it was impossible to know if she would stay in Aspen and if things would ultimately work out if she joined the firm, she assured me that no matter what happened, she would be fine, and we would be fine.

Hearing her optimism and flexibility made it easier for me to take a chance on her, because she understood and embraced the uncertainty of taking this sort of calculated risk. Luckily for both of us—and our team and all our clients—our partnership worked out beyond my greatest expectations. More than twenty years after joining as our sixth employee, she now serves as the president of OWP. Together with Dana Gleason Nightingale, our eleventh employee and current senior vice president, they form a majority of our leadership team. This positions OWP among the few top wealth management firms in the country with female leadership—a notable distinction in the financial services industry, where women hold just 18 percent of C-suite positions globally. Our leadership team is particularly significant in the traditionally male-dominated wealth management sector.

I've always run OWP as a meritocracy, and we've been extraordinarily fortunate to attract, hire, and retain leaders like Ali and Dana. It benefits both our team and our clients, as they represent the very clients we serve. Industry studies show that women are set to control much of the $30 trillion in financial assets baby boomers will possess by decade's end. With women making 85 percent of household spending decisions and positioned to inherit 70 percent of global wealth over the next two generations, OWP is strategically positioned to continue serving this growing market segment. Finally, as a father of three daughters, I take great pride in seeing women in deserved leadership positions.

Bringing Ali in cemented another critical aspect of what I think about when hiring: finding people with complementary skills—especially in those early years, skills that complemented my own. During the first six months of having her on board, it quickly became obvious that she was the yin to my yang: I was the big-picture person, and she was the make-the-big-picture-happen person. She rewrote our marketing brochure, reworked our website, and started a company newsletter. She even introduced us to PowerPoint, which, to her disbelief, we'd never used. One of her many strengths was being able to articulate our company's story in a way that resonated with clients, especially in meetings. This skill helped clients see the clear difference between our business philosophy and that of other wealth management firms. She had the vision for how we could improve ourselves, push ourselves, and scale ourselves—all aspects of growth that became particularly important when we merged with Wood Investment Counsel in 2014—and she had the ability to make it all happen. She understood how to integrate our firms and implement changes, big and small, to all our systems, including how to transition us from a small, family-run company with kids occasionally running around the office and new hires required to have dinner along with their current partner, if they had one, before offers were finalized. She helped us grow and change with grace so that we began to run things in a more traditionally professional way, all while keeping the best aspects of that small-company intimacy that made us who we were and who we always wanted to be.

There is a realistic bias that all finance people have a generic sort of look. If you attend any of the big finance conferences, you'll come away with a sense that the field is dominated by clean-cut, pinstripe-suited men with yellow or red Hermès ties. I am proud to say that OWP very intentionally does not fit that mold. I have already talked about my proclivity to hire people whose life stories have an interesting twist: We have a broad swath of clients whose lives couldn't be more different, which means they should be served by a team with a broad spectrum of interests and talents. We have created a culture at the firm that hopefully respects people's differences, and we work hard to pair clients with advisors who share their diverse interests. We have sophisticated urban art collectors and backcountry skiers, hunters and dedicated conservationists, people who have multiple graduate degrees and people who do not. I believe this gives our firm an advantage when we have the good fortune to have a new client walk in our doors. We can make sure they feel understood and connected with their client advisory team in a way the majority of people do not in a more traditional banking environment. Sometimes this takes time for our clients to become comfortable with. If they expect the blue suit and they get shorts and a ponytail or a fashionable woman or a bike racer, they might pause—but we have seen over time that having a diverse, interested, and interesting team builds strong and enduring relationships not only with clients but also among ourselves. The culture of the office is exciting and fun, and you never know what will happen next.

After experiencing during college and business school the notorious East Coast snobbishness that had rubbed me the wrong way, I developed a philosophy through working on the Vallecito Dam project that no one is above anyone else and everyone deserves to be treated with respect and kindness. That's how I view the world, and that's how I wanted to shape our firm: with people who embraced a flat hierarchical structure and checked their egos at the door.

This tendency can sometimes be taken to an extreme. When Helen came to see the new offices in Denver, I showed her around with great pride. We had beautiful artwork by renowned Colorado artists, a conference room that featured a spectacular fifteen-foot-long claro walnut table, and lovely offices with large windows framing the snow-covered peaks of the Rockies. As the tour continued, she got quieter and quieter. Finally, she turned to me and said, "But where is your office?" I took her there, and she stopped and stared at me. "You have got to be kidding," she nearly shouted. "Really, you have the Harry Potter closet under the stairs! Absolutely not! You are the president and chairman, and I am putting my foot down on that decision." Well, she wasn't wrong, and it was impressed upon me by my employees that clients might not even understand that logic—after all they expected a leader, not a mouse. Architects were called, and the office space was resolved, and I too ended up with a nice view and an office I enjoyed inviting clients and employees to meet with me in.

But I have never been comfortable thinking of myself as better than. No matter where I am or what I'm doing, whether at work or outside of the office, I always try to say hello to everyone, not just people in leadership or powerful positions but also those in support roles who do so much of the heavy lifting of keeping the world running. Whether it's the hostess at a restaurant, the receptionist at a doctor's office, or the mechanic at the airport, I address people by name upon arriving and leaving and thank them for whatever help or kindness they showed me. I've always practiced this with my team members too, especially with the junior ones, taking the time to sit with them to learn about their lives, families, aspirations, and fears.

I've been ribbed about how much time I've spent researching and interviewing prospective hires, to the point where one of our team members told me that her brother was convinced that she was trying to get a job with the CIA, not with a boutique wealth management firm in Aspen. Guilty as charged, but I want to know as much as I can about a person and about our compatibility—how we see the world and move through it— before committing to hiring them. This is why I make sure that one of our interview meetings always takes place in a restaurant or public space. I want to observe how they treat people whom they think they'll never see again—waiters, doormen, valets, cashiers. Again, respect for others is everything to me, as is the belief that no one within a company should feel too good to perform any task. I remember when I first offered Ali the job, I tried to talk her out of it multiple times because I wanted to be sure she understood that this would be something quite different from the big New York firms she'd worked for—she would be loading the copy machine and making coffee, just like the rest of us! No matter how many times I tried to scare her off, though, she insisted that Obermeyer was where she wanted to be because she wanted exactly that kind of intimate experience with team-mates and clients: a place where titles didn't matter and no one felt above anyone else, despite what might be on their résumé.

The two biggest mistakes I made in hiring over the years were the result of ignoring my gut about whether candidates were likely to evolve into good team members. Impressive résumés, social connections, and recommendations of friends don't supersede hard work, strong character, and the desire to do right by colleagues and clients. One of the hardest parts of running a business is when you realize you've made a mistake in a hire: that you've lost faith in them and have to take action to course-correct. I have always disliked that aspect of management the most, and I'd say it is truly one of my biggest challenges as a leader.

A flat hierarchical structure shaped the company from day one. In those early years, when we were small enough and I had the time, I did all the initial meetings with clients and often walked them through our paperwork myself. Having the founder of the firm personally and directly involved in client service seemed to me to be one of the most effective ways to prove our commitment to them and to our relationship. While I had to make certain adjustments in using my time as we grew, I never stopped prioritizing my close connection to the people we serve—I wanted our clients to know that if they had questions or concerns, they would always know where to find me: down the hall with my office door always open.

I may not have known a lot at the very beginning when I started Obermeyer Asset Management—now Obermeyer Wealth Partners—but one thing I did know with certainty was that I wanted to create the kind of investment management company that I would want for myself and my family: one that would be protective of a client's finances, that understood and balanced a person's tolerance for risk with their desire and need for growth, and that provided advice and counsel to preserve a person's lifetime of stored labor. More than anything, I wanted it to feel personal—for clients and for me. I wanted to get to know our clients fully so that I could assure them that our knowledge and understanding of who they were—where they'd come from, what challenges they were facing, where they hoped to go in the future—was just as necessary as our knowledge and understanding of the financial world. I wanted our small, independent firm of fiduciaries to be fully committed to a client-first mentality—not just because it was our legal duty to do so, but because that's who we would be and that's what we would believe in. Our core values would be woven into everything we would do for the people who trusted us with their money and the future of their families.

That said, I also wanted to be fully committed to the well-being of our precious team—the firm's lifetime of stored labor—which has meant prioritizing their needs too, something I'll discuss more in another chapter. We haven't done it very often, but there have been times when I've decided that the best thing we can do for ourselves is to turn a client away because it was clear that we wouldn't be a good fit. I remember once meeting with someone who, in the first few minutes of our first conversation, told me about how many people she was suing. Litigious people are never happy, and trying to make them happy only leads to trouble. Adding a client like that is never fair; our team's time is and should be limited to serving those who know and appreciate our value and trust that we're doing the absolute best for them. Dealing with a client who isn't going to respect us or our efforts is a waste of everyone's time and a depletion of our most precious natural resources: energy, enthusiasm, and spirit.

We've developed and refined our eight core values over the

years—*Integrity, Perseverance, Humility, Grace, Empowerment, Inge-nuity, Team Over Individual,* and *Thrive*—and while that list has never explicitly included another rule inspired by the advice of Stanford business school professor Robert I. Sutton in *The No Asshole Rule: Building a Civilized Workplace and Surviving One That Isn't,* when I read the book I realized that we've always instinctively followed that advice at OWP. If a client isn't the right fit, then no matter what we do, we'll ultimately disappoint them—or they'll disappoint us by making it impossible for us to help them. Maybe I should talk to Ali about adding that as our official ninth core value. And *Aspiring to Swing* as our tenth.

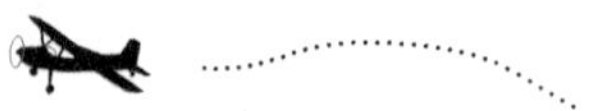

# THE HANDOFF: WHY
# COMMUNICATION IS EVERYTHING

When pilots transition an aircraft from one air traffic controller to another, we do what's called a handoff, a verbal directive that makes it clear who has control of the airplane. A handoff can also happen between a pilot and a copilot: If I were flying with someone and needed to take a break, I would say, "Your airplane." They would reply, "My airplane." The handoff is articulated. The situation is clear. No one is thinking or assuming something that's incorrect.

I remember learning about the importance of direct communication as a teenager, when I worked in the warehouse of Sport Obermeyer pulling orders for Sportana, the first sun protection of its kind for high altitudes like Aspen, which my dad had helped develop and which I mentioned in an earlier chapter. One of the orders I was tasked with filling for a customer had the number *24* handwritten on the form. Since we sold the lotion by the dozen, I dutifully pulled twenty-four boxes of that item, which meant twenty-four *dozen* bottles, or 288 bottles, filling up an entire huge shipping cart. The warehouse manager looked at me, then looked at the form, and said, with equal parts disbelief and annoyance, which I totally deserved: "Well, Wally, that's what it *says*. But does that actually make sense? Why don't you go call the customer and check?" That taught me to question things—like the absurdity of pulling 288 bottles of suntan lotion for a single order—and that a simple call to talk to someone directly is common sense and can make all the difference. That's why I'm often amazed at how many clients have come to us complaining about how the firms they worked with prior to coming to us did not clear that lowest bar of customer service—something as simple and basic as returning phone calls. Communication begins with answering the phone, returning phone messages, and replying to emails within a set time frame—something we've incorporated into our menu of best practices—and it extends far beyond that, including how we talk and listen to our clients during stressful times of change and transition. The substance of our work goes far beyond that—just like with children, spouses, friends, and colleagues, our relationships are built on trust, one conversation at a time.

People are very vulnerable when they come to us. Talking about money and finances is deeply personal, and it requires a person willing to listen to and share in understanding all of their ups and downs. People often equate who they are with how much money they have; we often draw conclusions about our standing in life relative to our financial standing. But wealth isn't just about money, as I'll talk more about in a later chapter. Wealth is also about personal satisfaction and human connection to friends and family, to community, to the greater good, and that's what we're there to talk about. We want to know and understand the full picture of someone's life so far—what they've done, what they've accomplished, the challenges they've faced along the way—and their hopes and dreams and concerns for the future. Maybe they're worried about the environment, and they want ESG (environmental, social, and governance) investing. In certain cases, it's more about asking somebody their long-term dreams and goals and what they want for their children. Understanding how they feel about their right to wealth versus their privilege of being wealthy is another subtle and helpful clue to who they are. We're trying to invest for a wide variety of people—often a multigenerational family—so being aware of all the concerns, attitudes, and feelings about a range of issues informs our investment advice and allows us to add value to their lives.

I go into every initial meeting wanting to know who someone is, how they got to where they are, what they love about their life, and what scares them the most. What I want to understand is often broader than the basic investment questions we cover, so I'll often ask people how they grew up, what their parents did, what their early economic life was like, how their families shaped them and their careers, and their feelings around risk and optimism. Those answers are usually incredibly revealing and give me a much fuller and richer sense of who someone is: how they relate to money and finances and how they've dealt with important issues throughout their life. An important part of the process is simply to get people talking. But talking about these topics is hard for a variety of reasons, including that people often feel they have to account for what they perceive are their mistakes or failures. One thing that helps lower the temperature of vulnerability is for us to make it clear that our life experience is equal to our financial expertise. An entrepreneur who just sold their business will likely feel anxious about not getting a regular paycheck, and because we've seen this or been through this ourselves, we'll make sure they get a distribution each month. If they've recently retired, we know that feeling productive enough will be a concern, so we'll help them find ways to do the things they've always been too busy to do. We've seen enough people facing similar changes, and we ourselves have likely gone through, and survived, similar ups and downs—of career shifts, divorces, illnesses, losses of loved ones—so creating an environment in which to share insecurities, vulnerabilities, disappointments, hopes, and ambitions is what we strive for. Isn't that what we all strive for in our relationships, business and personal?

Sometimes I'll ask what seems like an odd question in an otherwise business-focused meeting. I'll want to know about someone's favorite hobbies; where they like to go when they travel and what they love to do in their spare time; what they're most concerned about with respect to their children. Where people stand politically has become even more crucial given the current level of polarization, and it's important to know where those sensitivities are. Through those questions I may learn how someone thinks in terms of particular issues and investments as well as more general information: Do they want to buy NVIDIA at three hundred times earnings, or do they want something that's trading at ten times earnings, because it's cheap? During the last downturn, did they see that as an opportunity or a threat? What is their overall balance sheet? What are their income sources? What do they spend, and how much cushion do they have? Is being charitable important to them? If they don't have enough cushion on their taxable accounts, are they open to thinking longer term on their retirement accounts? Getting to know a client's overall financial picture is as important as understanding their investment personality.

Communication isn't just about talking, it's also about listening, so making sure that everyone is heard—especially each person in a couple or family—is another aspect of communication that we prioritize. Sometimes we meet one-on-one with a client; other times, a couple or multigenerational family members will be in the room together. Regardless of who's in the room, we want each person to be part of the conversation, and we never let a meeting end without making sure that everyone had their questions answered and their objectives noted, and that they're leaving with a complete understanding of all the concepts and plans discussed. We also want to create a time and a place where sensitive family issues and feelings can be expressed. I remember a particular moment during a conversation with a four-generation family when I asked everyone in the room to share the value they felt represented their family best. One of the daughters of the primary investor admitted that her father had always said to her, "No one ever remembers who came in second." This was a complete surprise to him, and what followed was a frank and open conversation about their family's ethos, which eventually led them to a better place of understanding, the way hard conversations do. Talking in the meeting that day softened her dad, cleared the air, and gave them an opportunity to think about their family legacy through a very different lens.

Meeting with couples is a particular challenge. Generally, it's the opinion of the quieter member of that couple that is very important to understand, and to dig into, because they're the one who could get lost in the conversation. Frequently, it's the husband who comes in and tries to drive the discussion, and it's very important then to notice that dynamic and listen to the quieter spouse by asking them, "How do you feel about that? What are your concerns? What's on your mind, and from your standpoint, what's been missed? What's important for us to know?" That's critical for us to elicit and hear. In fact, while the wife might ask questions, oftentimes the husband will answer, explaining investment products incorrectly. By which I mean he'll be wrong, and I'll very nicely try to correct him. Navigating conversations with couples is especially delicate and complex if one person isn't earning or hasn't had as lucrative a career as the other; it's important to hear from both people because both voices matter. The stay-at-home person is helping the person who's working and taking care of things at home, so together they're both contributing to make things work. Part of our job is to be sure that everyone's contribution is honored and that everyone's feelings are heard and considered in future decision-making. I remember a meeting with a couple where the husband dominated the conversation and answered all the questions directed to his wife. Two hours after they'd left, she called me and said, "Wally, get our finances in order. I need the name of a good divorce lawyer." I intentionally stalled in getting her that information, hoping things might cool down between them, and they did. Two weeks later when the three of us met again, we had a much more productive conversation because this time the husband did not do all the talking. I'm happy to report that they're still married and still working to have a more equal say in life planning and the financial decision-making processes.

Whether we're with individuals or couples, new clients or long-standing multigenerational family members, we always try to explain complex concepts and ideas in plain and simple language. The finance industry loves its acronyms, and it loves making things seem overly complicated, perhaps to intimidate clients into agreement because they're too embarrassed to ask for more information or explanations or admit they don't understand what the advisor is saying. Some people love talking P/E multiples, Sharpe ratios, and such things—they enjoy slipping into our technical language and feeling fluent in it—but most clients want straight talk, information and reassurance delivered through a conversation they can follow. I'll always try to come up with a story or a vocabulary that's particularly relevant or relatable: If someone loves flying the way I do, for instance, I'll talk about financial concepts and planning in terms of pilots' checklists for safeguarding against errors; if I'm with a real estate developer or someone who has worked in that area, I'll highlight that we're taking the same sort of risks but with different markers and measurements of returns and losses. Finding a shared language is key to helping people ride out difficult markets or to keep them from overextrapolating when things are positive.

Where I meet with a client often sets the tone of the relationship and can make a conversation more conducive to depth and connection. Most local clients like coming to the office in Aspen or Denver because they like seeing where and how we work—visualizing things makes them more comfortable—but meeting elsewhere is a better fit for others. For instance, I've had wonderful client meetings at Centennial Airport in Denver, which has a diner that overlooks the runway, the Denver Museum of Nature and Science, the Denver Art Museum, and the John Denver Sanctuary along the river near our Aspen office. And obviously in Aspen, there's always the option on a great skiing day to meet on the mountain and talk on the chairlift. Sometimes simply being out of the office and surrounded by nature or art or other distractions helps people relax and open up. For those who need privacy, we're willing to meet wherever they suggest, in their homes or their offices, no matter where they live; as I've mentioned, I'm only too happy to have an excuse to fly to them. I remember flying down to Midland, Texas, once to meet a prospective client at their local diner—they'd heard about us through word of mouth, and it was worthwhile to make that trip in order to prove our interest and commitment and to meet them on their own turf. There's something about going to a client's house that goes beyond the effort of travel: It's the willingness to be in their space, to hear them, to serve them by making things easier logistically on their side. I've often gone to see somebody at the hospital, to bring them paperwork to sign or because they were worried about something at that point in time. Again, we're dealing with people, and we're dealing with their life savings and the future of their families. If you're willing to parachute in and help them in their time of need, or to meet them on their own terms, it's incredible how it builds and deepens an existing relationship.

Curiosity is at the heart of connection, and I'm a big believer in the idea that talking less and listening more is the best way to give someone the space to tell their story. Some firms use a form or written questionnaire for new clients to fill out, asking them to indicate on a scale of one to ten how important a particular issue is to them, but I start each first conversation in person with a blank sheet of paper—literally. I want to ask questions and hear someone's answers. I take notes on a pad because I tend to listen better when I write things down, and because I want to make sure I capture nuances of what people are saying and sometimes not saying. This might seem old-school to some people, but being a keen and active listener helps me understand who a client is and what they need.

If we're lucky, and we have been, client relationships are long-lasting and full of moments when it's just as important for us to talk as it is for us to listen. An advisor who has the willingness to be open and vulnerable will benefit their clients greatly. Sometimes when I meet with people who are going through a divorce, for instance, I'll be honest about how I got through mine, what helped me and what didn't, and I'll assure them that they'll get through theirs too. If someone has lost a loved one and is struggling with grief, we let them know that we've seen this with other clients and have likely been through similar losses ourselves. We know how difficult life can be at times, and we believe that there's a comfort in talking about our experiences and in knowing that, just like the markets, while our lives go up and down, they always recover. Handing off problems to us and knowing that they're ours to take care of before handing them back in better shape is part of the journey we make together.

If we have done our jobs well, if we as a team are working together behind the scenes to make sure everything runs smoothly, doing our best to anticipate your needs, and doing the research and analysis to achieve the results that will give you the peace of mind you deserve, then we have achieved swing and are off the runway and in the air. That is the true spirit of lift.

# HOPE, OPTIMISM, RISK, AND TRUST

Helen admonishes me about my more recent tendency to look at my iPad and read headlines before bed. Knowing about this marital issue, a friend sent us a *New Yorker* cartoon depicting a couple in bed; the woman's caption reads, "Don't worry. Things will be much worse in the morning." My response is that I'm usually so busy at work that I often don't get to see the headlines of the day. That is only partially true: The rest of it has to do with the fact that I have been particularly stressed about the current political climate and the direction the country seems to be headed in. Having grown up in a family that has seen firsthand how authoritarianism led to catastrophic outcomes for the general population, I'm deeply concerned about where our current administration is taking us. The economic engine of the United States has always benefited from a strong middle class, but the vast discrepancy in wealth in the country now is quite worrisome. Politics is not my area of expertise, but when it's so significantly impacting the economy and all aspects of our society and culture, I feel I need to read the headlines, even if I do so while hiding under the covers so Helen doesn't catch me.

We're all wired a little differently, and investing takes a combination of faith and patience and a sense of belief in a better future. I've found in the investment management business that a very helpful question to ask clients is "Do you think the world will be better ten or fifteen years from now than it is today? Or in fifty years? Do you think your children or grandchildren will be in a better world?" If someone says yes, then they tend to be optimistic with a relatively high tolerance for risk. That means they're likely to be a more patient equity investor and more able to ride through market downturns because on some level they understand that markets always go down but they also always recover. In the same way, I have full faith that our democracy will hold and the political turmoil we are witnessing now will resolve, because I believe that, deep down, Americans are proud of our system of governance and will not let our country be overtaken by despots, despite a period of frustration about their personal circumstances. As Winston Churchill may or may not have said, "Americans can always be trusted to do the right thing, once all other possibilities have been exhausted." Though I worry, I also trust that the future is bright, that we're still innovating and creating growth opportunities at a historic rate, and that investing in the future is a sound idea.

Not everyone believes what I do. I have a client who is perhaps one of the smartest guys I know but one of the worst investors, because for him the world is always falling apart. As soon as the market goes down, his perception on how he views the world is validated. How someone sees the future reveals their level of hope and optimism, and knowing that is extremely helpful to me in terms of understanding who they are and how comfortable, or uncomfortable, they are likely to be with risk so that we can take the right approach with them. Past behavior is often more revealing about future behavior; everyone likes to think they're comfortable taking chances, but pushing back a little will reveal a more accurate answer. With someone of a certain age, I'll ask, "How did you and how did your portfolio do in 1999 and 2000?" Or "How did you handle 2008?" If they say, "We were fine, we were pretty conservative going into it, and we had plenty of cushion and we even bought more during the downturn," that's different from someone who says, "Oh, we liquidated everything. We just couldn't afford to lose any more money—and sleep." Knowing someone's level of comfort (or discomfort) with uncertainty helps us advise them and craft a strategy that suits their needs and their personality. We want to protect and grow our clients' wealth, and we also want to make sure they can sleep at night. It's this kind of information that helps us craft an investment strategy that is right for them.

We always invite our clients to think long-term when it comes to growing their investment portfolio. Because we're able to manage things over time and have lived through many ups and downs, we can try to insulate people from their own worst tendencies: to liquidate during downturns, or to feel overwhelmed by anxiety, or to chase last year's hottest portfolio, which will likely be one of the lesser investments the next year. Understanding the impact of volatility on a portfolio is important: For instance, if you buy one hundred dollars of something that goes down 50 percent in the first year, you then need 100 percent return to get it back up. I always tell clients that I can guarantee that if they're with us long enough, there will be years when their equity portfolio will go down. While the Securities and Exchange Commission (SEC), appropriately, disallows wealth investors to promise returns, I promise some negative returns. Sometimes, after successfully guiding a client through a rough patch, they'll say, "Oh no, Wally, you were smart, and I wasn't afraid at all because you told me that we would have downturns." So in a funny way, we get credit for being right. But that requires that clients believe in us, and if they do, their faith that we can lead them through the long term to good results works for all of us.

Building wealth takes time. While some of it is luck, positive results are more typically the accumulation of a series of thoughtful decisions over time that work out incredibly well. It's always remarkable to me how hard people work in their careers to earn while at the same time managing to save. By being diligent about saving and thus having the opportunity to invest in good companies and ideas, some risky and some more conventional, they're able to help themselves and society at the same time. I'm moved by how admirable that balancing act is. Whether they're doctors or lawyers or accountants or ski patrolmen, I've seen some amazing results in the town where I grew up and where my practice is based. Many of our clients have bought land and homes and enjoyed huge escalation in Aspen pricing. Similarly, we've seen people who do all the right things, but circumstances beyond their control hinder a successful outcome. There is no surefire formula for success. Saving and investing and the miracle of compound interest are certainly much more likely to leave you with a substantial nest egg than spending, but still there are no guarantees. Most people who come to us have considerable assets to manage, people who have been successful and fortunate. Occasionally clients will come to us who have had poor investment advice or even, in the case of Madoff-type fraud, actual illegal investments. Those are always heartbreaking, as bad investments do lead to significant downturns. Generally, though, the people who come to us are conservative and are not looking for a home run. They have had real estate and business success, and they want to preserve it. In the Roaring Fork Valley where Aspen is, I often say that we're investing for the millionaires who've been bought out by the billionaires.

I've found that reframing a conversation about risk by making the case for cautious optimism and putting things into historical perspective can help enormously. Markets are going to rise and fall, and I always tell people that I can't guarantee anything, except that at some point, their accounts will be down. Clients often seem shocked when we admit that so matter-of-factly, but we're always shocked that more advisors aren't as transparent about the limitations of their skills—that we're all "cooking with water." There really isn't a secret formula to investing, and anyone who says there is shouldn't be trusted. Setting realistic expectations from the beginning and reminding clients that on average, markets are down one year out of every three—followed by however much time it takes for recovery—is critical. Using actual data to paint a fuller picture reassures them that they will get through whatever fluctuations come their way. Every down market is scary, but history has shown us that companies pivot and recreate themselves, and stock markets recover. Reminding people of the cyclical nature of things during difficult times and being willing to be there and have those hard conversations with them when things are tough can be an enormous comfort for them and can help them make good decisions. Many advisors put their heads in the sand or are scarce during difficult times. But to me, that's when we earn our stripes: being able to talk people through their situations and make sure that they're as comfortable as possible with uncertainty and that their anxiety doesn't cause them to make common mistakes that really could be detrimental for their long-term growth. One of the many reasons Warren Buffett is a successful, stable investor is that if you ask him how the world's going to be fifteen years from now or fifty years from now, he'll say, "Well, just look at the increase in wealth during my lifetime. Imagine what it will be fifty years from now." Cautious optimism like that is a great way to think about building wealth.

Another maxim of mine is always surprise your banker on the upside. If you build in enough downside in your modeling, if you under-promise and over-deliver, it won't be such a shock when a downturn happens—and it will happen. There will always be periods when the market fluctuates, and there will always be times when we underperform. Like most advisors, we want to make sure our clients are happy, but having difficult conversations about the market or our performance must take precedence over people-pleasing and over-promising. Two of my favorite expressions from studying economics are "God invented economists to make weathermen look good" and "A broken clock is right twice a day." In the wealth management business, there will always be people who predict a big market downturn or upturn, and when those things come true, they will have been right, temporarily. The psychology of investing is closely related to the psychology of the markets: If people think the economy is improving, they'll buy more, and the economy will improve.

The power of suggestion isn't everything, but it's certainly a strong force in perception and decision-making. *Same as Ever: A Guide to What Never Changes*, by former *Wall Street Journal* and *The Motley Fool* columnist Morgan Housel, talks about the notion that one thing that never changes is that we can't predict the future. None of us knows what it means until we look through the rearview mirror at the past. One thing that we do know, which would likely be on Warren Buffett's list, is that the economy will be larger on a per capita basis fifty years from now than it is today. When a recession will come, or how long it will last, we simply can't know—which is why we take time frames into account. If you have a minimum of three years, you can ride through most downturns. There have been very few five-year periods where the markets are down: In 90 percent of five-year periods, the market has been up. In constructing portfolios, we recommend building in a five-year cushion of potential withdrawals; this way, a client shouldn't need to sell long-term investments during challenging markets, and they should have a positive return over time.

Talking about risk wouldn't be complete without two of my favorite western-flavored expressions: "You can't get up early enough in the morning to deal with a crook," and the Texas saying, "Big hat, no cattle." You can learn a lot at business school, but what they don't teach you is how to become a good judge of character. I remember years ago, one of our clients asked me to suss out an investment run by someone who would end up going to prison for stealing. When I met with the advisor my client was excited about, I had an immediate negative feeling about him: He was just too perfect. There wasn't a scratch on his shoe; not a hair was out of place; the handkerchief in his vest pocket was absolutely perfect. It didn't sit well with me—nobody is that perfect—and it was obvious that he spent more time on his image than on what he was trying to sell to potential investors.

To the degree that picking up on dishonesty is instinctual, I encourage my team and my clients to pay attention to their gut when they sense something is off with potential investments or investors by asking themselves and each other, "How did you feel about that? Do you think that person was for real? What vibes did you get?" I may sometimes be wrong, but I never stop asking myself those questions—because along with the level of extreme wealth in Aspen has come a number of colorful grifters. Bernard Madoff had a significant impact on the overall per capita wealth of the town for a few years, and a fascinating podcast, *The Pirate of Prague*, tells the incredible story of Viktor Kožený, a Czech swindler who threw an epic Christmas party in 1997 at Peak Mansion (his $20 million, twenty-two-thousand-square-foot house at the top of Red Mountain) and hired actors as props in his international financing scam, then left town with several million dollars of other peoples' money.

In the old days for which Aspen is renowned, the appeal wasn't the ostentatious displays of wealth, the mega mansions on Red Mountain, and the airport full of Gulfstreams—it was the characters and personalities that the place attracted. Those were the days of musicians and writers, like John Denver and Hunter S. Thompson—I have many wonderful memories of my teenage years and my early twenties sitting around a campfire with John and friends, where everybody else was high and "seen it rainin' fire in the sky." While I didn't gravitate to the drug culture, and I didn't shoot shot glasses off fence posts with Hunter at his Woody Creek ranch, I did see some things back then—like the night I was barely out of the parking lot of the Aspen Club when the car that had been parked next to mine, owned by someone we ski patrollers referred to as "the man who skied like an ape," blew to smithereens with that man in it. He'd been expected to testify in court the next day on drug charges, and clearly one of his "business" associates didn't want that to happen. I also remember the night I was sound asleep in my trailer when the door was pried open with a tire iron. The next thing I knew, longtime Aspen local and ladies' man Jim Blanning was raging about how I'd "stolen" his girl. Well, "his" girl had a cast on at the time, and the girl in my bed did not, so he slunk away, and the next morning left me a bottle of whisky on the doorstep with a note of apology. Jim would later go on to place four pipe bombs around Aspen on New Year's Eve in 2008, causing the town to be evacuated and countless restaurants and bars to lose millions in holiday revenue, and leading to his screed about how the town had been turned into a playground for the rich.

A few of these characters and other ostensible "interested investors" have come my way over the years, people who didn't feel right to me, and who, when I dug deeper into their backgrounds, proved to be frauds, as I'd suspected. The investment community is rife with skimmers, scammers, and flimflammers, shady dealmakers paying for their larger-than-life lifestyles and putting their kids through school on the private equity fees from funds falsely promising extraordinary returns. For all its natural beauty, Aspen has a treacherous economic element running through it, a counterpoint that keeps us all on our toes. For those who think that moving here and living alongside the wealthy means that they too will become "rich," the reality is that more often than not the opposite happens: They can't afford the real estate or the lifestyle, and soon their entire savings have disappeared.

I always tell my team to not make snap judgments based on people's appearances. I remember walking with my wife, originally a New Yorker, to the movies one night and watching her navigate us away from a somewhat sketchy looking man on the sidewalk. After we passed him I whispered that she didn't need to worry about him as he was one of our wealthier clients. Similarly, some people who come to Aspen with entitlement and privilege treat those in the service industry extremely rudely. One woman who works in the restaurant business in town is often on the receiving end of this kind of behavior. Little do the people who barely give her the time of day know, though, that her investment portfolio with us is likely double theirs.

# SHARING JOY WITH A SERVICE HEART

Warren Buffett has always said that he loves what he does so much that he tap-dances to work each morning. He even wrote a book called *Tap Dancing to Work*. My guess is that people who are more successful in business tend to be those who really love what they do, and what those people most have in common is that they love their work because they know they're adding value to people's lives. It's the notion that the more you give, the more you receive; the more you help people, the more you get in the form of satisfaction and enjoyment. Doing good work for people makes you feel better.

This way of thinking affected me early on and became one of the core values of my own business. If one focuses on maximizing the value that can be added to the service or product being provided, there will be long-term positive effects for everyone involved. Short-term focus on maximizing earnings is one of the seamy sides of most businesses. There are many financial investors who don't care about the value of the relationships with the clients they're serving and are only concerned with their own immediate profits. In fact, most big investment houses only compensate their employees on new money brought into the firm, not on servicing existing funds under management. The reality is you can always make an extra dollar, but that isn't always what matters most. Plus, clients have a sense for that, and I believe it eventually hinders the long-term growth we are always focused on at OWP.

Over the years, we decided that creating even more dedicated and personalized service at Obermeyer Wealth Partners was one of our next priorities. Service, we realized, was tied to the notion of hospitality—of making clients feel welcome and appreciated and valued in every way possible. That's when Dana, who manages our advisory business, suggested hiring more team members from the hospitality industry. She found and hired Sean, who had been trained at the Ritz-Carlton. It seemed so obvious to Dana to bring in people trained in service by experts at companies that specialized in hospitality at the highest level. What he's done to create a sense of warmth and connection for clients and staff alike has changed our culture for the better. Talking about finances is stressful, and if we can make any part of that process easier and more pleasant—if we can create an experience that includes flowers and art and lunch served at a table set with plates and silverware by true professionals, with a beautiful view of the mountains—then we have literally set the table for service.

We want this to be an experience, not just a transaction, so every bit of contact with a client is an opportunity for personal connection. Our team is trained to give clients a warm welcome when they walk in, to recognize them not only while they're here but also when they run into them on the street or in the supermarket, and to send them off with a fond farewell when they leave. It matters how we answer the phone—if we do it with a smile, people can hear that warmth. We want to use a client's name as much as possible, even if we're just transferring a call; in person or on Zoom meetings, we want to look clients in the eye when they're talking, to not keep our head down when we're taking notes, to always ask before letting them go, "Have

I helped you with everything? Is there anything else you need?" Maybe someone is looking for a new CPA, or a good divorce lawyer, or someone to help with their kids, and if they are, we'll try to connect them with someone in the firm who can then connect them with the right person. We always thank people for calling, for reaching out, for their time, and for their business because we're grateful for all of it. We wanted our offices to truly feel like home, and now they do. If you've had a great lunch, and you've had a great meeting, and everything was beautiful, you're likely to be in a little bit better mood when you leave than when you walked in, and maybe because of that, you'll be more likely to say hello to someone you pass on the street or thank a person who helps or serves you. We're generating a good feeling that we hope carries through to the rest of someone's day, and that's a powerful thing for all of us. It's how we spread joy.

I remember once asking Sean why he does what he does, and why he loves it so much, and I've never forgotten his answer. "I have a service heart," he said, and that phrase—so simple and perfect—stuck with me. To him, having a service heart means being someone who anticipates others' needs and finds joy in making people happy, making their day just a tiny bit easier and more beautiful, treating people with respect and kindness always, and making people feel like family. I like to think we were the perfect culture match for him because while I'd never called it that, everyone at OWP has a service heart too. We hire for that—people who want to make clients feel like family, who want to make them feel seen and appreciated, who want to understand their personalities and quirks and hobbies, and who want to make people feel cared for when they come to see us. Sean's service heart may have come from his early life when he worked on his grandfather's ranch or helping his grandmother on the other side of his family with cleaning chores, and it endured, guiding his profession first at the Ritz-Carlton and now gratefully for us. His innate sense of wanting to please others has always been and will always be at the core of his life's work in the same way that it is for our company. Our service heart extends to all aspects of our clients' lives. Through newly created computer systems we mark birthdays and milestones and make note of our clients' hobbies and interests, recent trips they've taken, how their children and grandchildren are doing, what health challenges or life changes they might be going through. That's the psychology of hospitality—connection and caring and comfort—and client service is one of the most important things we do.

We're imparting our service heart to our clients, but it also extends to ourselves, which is one major difference between us and other wealth management firms. For one thing, we don't work on commissions, which means pay isn't based on products sold or new money brought into the firm. We believe enough in the people we hire to know that they will eventually bring in business and contribute in meaningful ways to the growth of the company without the pressure of making quotas. Being able to focus on the quality of our work and the quality of our client relationships is where we want our energy going. And because we hire for life, we take our investment in the people who form our team seriously. Generous compensation makes people feel valued and appreciated, so along with competitive salaries, top medical benefits, and flexible vacation and personal time to ensure that everyone is supported in big ways and small ways—from being able to take care of their families during times of illness or loss to being able to pick up their children from school or take sick pets to the vet—we make room for our employees to live their lives. Not holding to a strict corporate absence policy requires trust, and we have almost never felt that ours had been misplaced.

We also invest in the future of our team members by supporting them in pursuing additional business education and
advanced financial certifications. All these things are a way
for us to be there for each other because often we spend more
time with our office work families than with our actual families. That means being able to rely on each other and look to
each other for support and mentoring—which makes me think
about something that Skip Dines, a now-retired partner who
continues to serve on the executive committee in his emeritus
role, said about mentoring and helping newer team members
find their way in their careers. "Everyone needs a rock," he told
me. That's what he tries to be for those who need one, and that's
what we try to be for each other and for our clients. Because
even a rock needs a rock.

Internally, we're each other's clients, each other's family,
each other's rock. True service is a gift of kindness—not a
transaction—and when people are receiving kindness, they tend
to pay it forward and send it back out into the world.

# PROTECTING AND GROWING "THE MOTHER"

When I think about wealth, I think about my stepdaughter Kyra's metaphor for investing. She loves to bake. She taught me about "the mother"—not the human being, but the pre-fermented culture that's the foundation for sourdough bread—and how nurturing it is a bit like thinking about money. The mother starts with the basics—flour and water—and through careful management of that combination of basic elements, you can either continue to carefully grow it or carelessly destroy it. Managing money is much the same. It, too, is a living and breathing organic process that takes vigilance and respect to maintain. Each step of the way, over the course of years and years of studying the market and understanding each client's needs, we add and subtract ingredients, adjusting and readjusting our assessment for risk and profit, until we develop a system and a recipe that makes sense for each individual we serve. Over time, we've realized that the art and science of good investing requires patience, attention, and persistence, values that protect the integrity of a person's wealth and security.

I view people's wealth and savings as their stored labor. It may be that of their parents or their grandparents or an ex-spouse, but however it was acquired, it's still money that's been earned and not consumed. I always think about the labor that earned that money. Whether it's intellectual labor or physical labor, it's stored labor that needs to be protected. To remake that money would, for most of our clients, be almost impossible: They likely wouldn't be able to start over and duplicate the amount of luck, hard work, time, and the skill set that was relevant then but may be outdated now. That's why we're always trying to avoid a permanent loss of principal, which would mean a permanent loss of spending power, when you acknowledge the drag of taxes and inflation. At the risk of wondering if I should "block that metaphor" the way *The New Yorker* used to humorously advise, I think sticking with the bread-baking analogy for this works well to illustrate these basic ideas:

*Overheating*: Almost every time I've tried to make a quick buck with a scheme that seems too good to be true, it has resulted in a loss of the assets I put to work. I overheated, falling into a trap of thinking I knew more than I did or that the markets were not seeing something I could see, which caused me to bet too much. After years of experience, I've learned to be much more careful about taking undue risk and recognizing the moments of impulsivity that can lead to overheated thinking.

*Overcooling*: Being too cautious is almost as problematic. There have been many instances, particularly early on in my career, when I did the analysis, checked and rechecked my assumptions, and then either didn't pull the trigger or was too timid and didn't make a big enough investment, thus missing an important opportunity for significant growth. Trusting yourself and your research enough to take a calculated risk is one of the skills required for smart investing.

*Overfeeding*: I have made the mistake of being too committed to reinvesting without taking into consideration the very important idea of life balance. Overfeeding sometimes caused me to unwittingly hurt those around me because I was giving up too much of myself in the pursuit of more. The power of compounding interest can be a trap. At some point, you must live your life in the present and not be entirely dedicated to building for a bigger, better future.

*Underfeeding*: This is the more common mistake in wealth management and one that I don't have a proclivity for. You can't build wealth if you're always spending and taking away from the source of growth potential. I don't spend easily the way most people do. For some, wealth is a means to spend, and spending can become an obsession that can seriously undermine growth and security.

*Not Paying Attention*: Managing your money takes time and vigilance, rigor and commitment, and there are bound to be times when people are distracted and not paying active attention to their portfolio, hoping the status quo will endure. But markets are fickle, and companies go through good times and bad, and you'll likely benefit over the long term if you have someone vigilant helping you stay on top of these trends.

*Using It All Up*: As a manager of other people's wealth, this is what every advisor fears the most: the client who is clearly headed for financial disaster. Either their circumstances have changed, and they don't adjust their spending commensurate with a newer and lower income stream, or they have unexpected financial hardship and don't make the tough decisions necessary to compensate for it. Often, particularly in multigenerational scenarios where wealth is passed on, the beneficiaries do not have the same understanding of and respect for the time and effort it took to create their family's original wealth and thus are more profligate in their spending.

The ultimate goal in thinking about investing is much like the mother: You want to nurture it to the point that it gives you unlimited access to the outcome you are after: bread—pun intended! You want to get your portfolio to the point where your money works for you and starts growing rather than being your taskmaster. This is the ideal scenario, beyond living paycheck to paycheck, when someone has enough to invest: when the bills have been paid, a few indulgences have been accounted for, savings for retirement and education have been attended to, and your home is financially secure. When people reach the point of having the privilege and opportunity to figure out what to do with the rest of their money, that is the time clients come to us looking for help and advice.

As they should. Money that is invested prudently becomes an engine for creating true wealth. True wealth is not the balance in your bank account for day-to-day expenses, but rather the money you put aside to work for you through investments, as opposed to money that disappears elusively into the ether. There are always times when luck and timing play a role in whether investments pay off or not, when you will lose money and you'd hoped to make it, but having faith and trusting in the fact that, over time, good companies and good managers will prevail and keep the nest egg growing is what smart investing is all about. Investing in good companies is a virtuous circle. By giving those companies the opportunity to grow further, you get to go along for the ride and reap the benefits; their success is your success.

Finding an advisor who values honor and integrity more than anything else is one of the most important things you can do to ensure your financial security for generations to come. People measure wealth in different ways, and the act of measuring it can become an obsession and an addiction in and of itself. Many people sacrifice everything in their pursuit of more, unable to control their insatiable appetite to compete with and outperform those around them, and countless good investors with good strategies blow up their businesses by over-leveraging, using derivatives and option strategies to accelerate their gains—strategies that more often than not end up in disaster, causing people to lose exponentially.

I've now spent most of my professional life building a registered investment advisory business. I've studied economics as an undergraduate and gone to business school, read far too many books about finance and investing, and absorbed hundreds of thousands of articles and newsletters about investment analysis, structuring portfolios, and managing assets for myriad individual life scenarios. I know countless people in the industry, some good, some not so good, some shockingly and dangerously bad, and I've had deep conversations with all of them about how they approach the business and how they think about investing. I've seen people's lives destroyed or transformed for good through wealth. I've watched people obsess over a basis point in return and watched investors fire manager after manager for underperforming an index they don't even understand, then witnessed them consistently sell at the bottom and buy near the top. And I've seen people destroy themselves and their sense of peace, fighting through lawyers to ensure that a family member or ex-spouse doesn't get an extra cent of what they consider to be their money.

As I mentioned at the beginning of this book, what continues to interest me most in the work I do with my team is the core question of how we ultimately define money, wealth, and success. Why do we work so hard to earn money, and what does financial success actually mean to us? Wealth is, in my opinion, overly correlated with success in the United States. Americans are bombarded with images of success from a young age; we're sold on the notion that bigger is better, that luxury brands not only confirm our sense of success but telegraph it to others. Projecting the image of success takes work, and many people create undue stress on themselves and their families by making more only to spend more. This is the vicious cycle of the pursuit of wealth, not the virtuous circle of smart investing.

But in many ways, money and wealth are an illusion, a construct of safety and protection and future security that we've accepted as fact and that doesn't exist. We believe in the absolute value of money, of the dollar, and yet that value often is not as solid as it seems. Ask anyone from Venezuela, where hyperinflation between 2016 and 2018 reached 100,000 percent and where it has cooled off to a mere 200 percent today. The actual value of their money turned out to be smoke. The bolivar doesn't buy anything now, and many Venezuelan families who once had significant wealth are currently facing true financial hardship. This happened through no fault of their own, but despite believing in their government's regulations and following the rules, their savings are gone and they're struggling day-to-day to provide for their families' most basic needs.

Another example takes place much closer to home. An article about recent wildfires included a description of a home that was destroyed: one with eighteen bedrooms, two pools, an underground temperature-controlled wine room, a gym, a twenty-person theater, and two panic rooms. Whoever owned that house had built themselves a palace with elements of a fortress, where they thought they'd be safe and protected. The act of building one of the biggest houses in one of the most expensive neighborhoods in the country is a statement, one that is meant, consciously or unconsciously, to project an image of wealth and success. I don't doubt that the owner of this house worked incredibly hard, and I have no problem with their wanting others to admire their success, but in the end, that house, like so many others, burned to the ground. Now they'll be lucky to get a small percentage of what they spent to build it back from insurance. Even if they do get a significant reimbursement, that neighborhood and all that it represents has disappeared, at least for the next decade or so. Land values will be a fraction of what they were before and will stay that way for a long while.

So what happened? Forces beyond our control can make wealth disappear overnight. Stories like this abound, from natural disasters to people who buy once-hot art or cars or jewelry or horses that turn out to be out of favor when they eventually try to sell them. As a wealth manager who has spent my whole life helping clients feel secure by helping them build wealth, thinking deeply about my own relationship to wealth and the sense of security that growing and preserving it brings to me and my family, I know how important the breadth of one's definition of wealth can be. Financial wealth is transitory, temporary; as easy as it can come, it can also disappear.

I've always believed that beyond the essential level of financial security that we all need to survive and thrive, what matters most is emotional and personal wealth: the bonds and connections we build through friends, family, and community. Tending to the growth of wealth and being an investment advisor feels to me very much like creating and maintaining the mother. With constant vigilance and committed care, the results can be miraculous. Just like maintaining a sourdough mother for baking, preserving an essential level of financial security needed to survive and thrive means avoiding actions that can jeopardize the health and well-being of a client's lifetime of stored labor and focus. Our goal is to create an environment for our clients in which true wealth—emotional contentment and financial security—can be self-sustaining.

# FLYING LESSONS:
## PREPAREDNESS, COMPLIANCE, AND RESPECTING THE RULES

It's always interesting to me how scared people are of flying in general and of flying in small planes in particular. While it's true that there are more accidents in small planes than in commercial aircraft, relative to car accidents there is no comparison. Statistics from the National Transportation Safety Board for 2022 show this: Nineteen people died in air accidents, of which 27 percent were on commercial flights and 73 percent were general aviation. Passenger car and truck accidents during the same time period totaled 552,009 deaths. Or, according to the Colorado Airport Operators Association, your odds of dying in a plane crash are one in 11 million versus one in five thousand in a car crash.

If you listen to airplane accident reports the way I compulsively do, mechanical problems are exceedingly rare. Almost all accidents are pilot error, due to what I call "get there-itis." Putting yourself and others in a position in which you feel you absolutely must get somewhere can kill you. No meeting or holiday is so important that you should fly in unsafe conditions, particularly in this day and age when Zoom meetings are an option and most weather systems will only delay your holiday plans by a day or so. The piloting community understands the adage "If you have time to spare, go by air"—they know that weather, mechanical issues, and a pilot's ability to fly can prevent taking off and thus delay travel. Having acceptance and patience is the surest way to guarantee you get where you're going safely. I'll never forget watching a plane come into Montrose during a snowstorm. The plane was encrusted in ice. Ice on the wing is one of the scariest situations for a pilot. It interrupts the flow of air over the wing and prevents the lift that makes flying possible. The man who had piloted the plane to pick up his family quickly loaded them and took off. His total disregard for safety enraged me, and all of us who witnessed that terrible spectacle held our breath as the plane miraculously climbed out without falling from the sky.

Despite taking safety very seriously, I, too, have occasionally ended up in some uncomfortably challenging situations. I had probably made over a hundred trips to Bozeman, Montana, when one cloudy winter morning Helen and I took off from Aspen in the Cessna 180. As I mentioned before, the Cessna does not have deicing equipment, but I had thought I could scud run the clouds, meaning they would be far enough apart for me to be able to see ahead and avoid them. The farther we went, though, the more the clouds were socked in and the more ice we picked up on the wings. There was no place to land, and no going back, and all we could do was power through and hope we'd make it. Luckily, right before our situation became an emergency, we broke out of the clouds, and the sun and temperature worked quickly to melt the ice off the wings. We should never have taken off, of course, but the pressure I had felt to get to Bozeman led me to make a very poor decision.

Sometimes it's luck that saves you. I had flown to almost every Berkshire Hathaway meeting in Omaha over the past fifteen years, usually with a few team members or clients, and had never had a problem. But one year in the 414, worried that I might not have enough fuel to make it all the way, I stopped at a little airport outside Chicago. When I went to inspect the plane before taking off again, I noticed I was down nine quarts of oil. Unbeknownst to me, there was a mechanical issue causing the plane to drain oil. Had I continued straight without stopping to refuel, we'd have definitely needed to make an emergency landing. Thankfully, there have only been a few of these incidents, but the lessons I learned flying have been some of the strongest ones I use in all aspects of my life.

Preparedness is applicable to all aspects of life, and with flying it's essential, though just when you think you've considered every possible scenario, you'll still be surprised by the unexpected—another perfect metaphor for life. If there's one thing I can point to that I've instilled in my team, it's the value of slowing down and doing a good job. As a pilot, I've always believed in the power and sanctity of the checklist, which is essentially about coming up with and adhering to processes and practices that ensure accuracy and safety. No matter how many times I've flown, no matter how well I knew my processes and procedures, I never once skipped my checklists, or skipped having the person flying next to me in the right seat help me with checklists. I even made *The Checklist Manifesto: How to Get Things Right*, by the brilliant surgeon, writer, and public health advocate Atul Gawande, required reading within the firm.

Whenever we've come up with a process at OWP, we've transformed it into a checklist form. From signing up new clients to going through all aspects of managing their investments and accounts, rules must be followed, and nothing can fall through the cracks. Most of our checklists are automated in the form of software and technology, which simulates the checklist process by walking us all through various series of questions and tasks to complete, but the essence remains the same: Making sure we're taking care of our clients in the best way possible begins and ends with preparedness, safety, and compliance. And at the core of the checklist is trust: We want our clients to feel like they're in the best hands on our flight together, that their safety is our utmost priority, and that the work we'll do on their behalf will lead them to a safe landing at a better place. The trust our clients place in us to protect and steward their savings, the assurance that they're in good hands, is everything. I recently received a note that said, "We so appreciate your team because we don't have to worry. Thank you for relieving us of all those pressures in the world that we don't have to think about." That sort of response not only feels amazing to read, but we also understand the bigger-picture meaning of those words: With trust comes a tremendous amount of responsibility. We don't ever want to violate that trust. Our working capital is our reputation. And that reputation can be lost in an instant.

One of the best articulations of this point comes from Warren Buffett's testimony before Congress in September 1991 when he took over Salomon Brothers during a securities scandal: "Lose money for the firm, and I will be understanding," he said. "Lose a shred of reputation for the firm, and I will be ruthless." I always play this clip at our annual retreat and often at home. Every time I hear it, it gives me goose bumps, because that fundamental value is so absolute and purely stated. Everyone at OWP internalizes and upholds that standard. Again, our reputation is our working capital, and that is the bottom line for all of us.

In terms of compliance and safety, I believe the government has done a particularly good job with the Federal Aviation Administration (FAA). The insurance industry has also provided phenomenal oversight to the airlines, and especially with private charter operators. They are tighter regulators, believe it or not, than the FAA, which protects us all. I'm a big believer in regulations, in retraining, and in the redundancy that is either encouraged or mandated by those regulations. Those things keep us safe in the air and on the ground. Rules have promoted success in several areas I've worked in, including the hydroelectric project, which is on a Bureau of Reclamation project, requiring that our equipment, our installation, and our regulation of the water flow through the dam does not damage the dam or their equipment or jeopardize the safety of anyone downstream. Respecting their jurisdiction and that of the other regulators—the US Fish and Wildlife Service, Colorado Parks and Wildlife, and FERC—is extremely important, and following those regulations has allowed us to do a much better job being a partner on this project.

With respect to the financial business, I've always felt that the SEC is our friend, not our foe. I think of how much worse things would be without financial regulation in this country— the potential for chaos and fraud would increase exponentially. Most of the SEC regulations are rules that we should follow anyway because they're good business practices: keeping copies of emails, keeping a list of customer complaints and how we've resolved them, not making promises about performance, guarding our clients' private information and financial data. These are already a part of our compliance efforts.

Some see the IRS as the enemy, rather than our friends that help society work better. In my view, if there's good tax compliance on what's owed, then I may even have to pay less. A certain number of people need a stick, rather than a carrot, to do the right thing, but we don't. That's why we decided back in 2017 to hire someone solely devoted to compliance, thereby making a meaningful investment of resources in this aspect of our business. When Charlton Rugg answered our LinkedIn ad for a chief compliance officer position, he was taking a leap by applying. He had been a lawyer in private practice at the famed white-shoe law firm Simpson Thacher & Bartlett LLP, he'd worked at the Department of Justice, and he'd worked at the Financial Industry Regulatory Authority, a private not-for-profit organization responsible for protecting investors by ensuring investment firms comply with regulations. He'd seen the financial industry from the regulatory side, and I knew after meeting with him several times that our visions in this area matched up: I was serious about compliance and so was he.

There's a common feeling in the business world, especially across financial services, that compliance is the "business impediment department"—that companies comply because of the SEC, and that they'll go through the performative motions of following the rules without actually internalizing them. Charlton may have heard me say all the right things during our interviews and conversations, but he had come from the DOJ, where one of their mottos, he told me, was "trust but verify"— which he did when we started working together. He knew that I had been struck by Warren Buffett's testimony in Congress and the idea that you can spend twenty years building a reputation and lose it in five minutes. He knew that clients would tolerate a lot of things, including losing money in tough markets or bad calls when we've bought securities that didn't perform the way we hoped they would, either because we missed something, or the story about the company changed, or the market never saw what we thought we saw. And he knew that what they absolutely would not tolerate were questions around integrity. Investment decisions needed to be viewed through three lenses—law, ethics, and optics—like the time we were considering a particular investment in the cannabis space. Were we legally allowed to support this kind of business? As fiduciaries, with a duty to steward our clients' money, was this a prudent investment for them? And from an optics perspective, would our clients appreciate an investment in this area? The aperture of the compliance lens can be quite wide when it comes to these sorts of questions and decisions.

Compliance has gotten a bad rap over the past few decades—the business world has convinced the American public that government is harmful or useless at best and that free markets are the only possible solution to any problem. This tenet is embedded into the society and culture in a very broad and deep way that has produced a resistance to and resentment of rules and regulations: When a president says that cheating on his taxes makes him smart, it sends the message that rules are for chumps. But rules are important. Rules were created to protect us all—workplace safety standards, labor laws, environmental regulations—though the protective aspect is less obvious when it comes to securities regulation. Money doesn't seem harmful, but what happens around money can be, especially around fraud and market manipulation and the desperation of people who are victimized by predators and scammers. These regulations also provide the framework in which everything we do exists. When we're stewarding our clients' money, we need to do that within a set of expectations and rules that everybody is playing by. Because when people break the rules, it becomes impossible to assess an investment accurately, which is how we got the kinds of massive accounting frauds we've seen in the last twenty years.

I've always believed in the ideas that capitalism is good at growing the pie for everybody and that we need to take care of people—and that those ideas are not mutually exclusive. Or, they don't have to be. There has never been a purely free market, and regulating markets is, from an antitrust perspective, the way to curb the accumulations of power, to make sure money is more evenly distributed. We could have capitalism and still have a society that takes care of people—we've had that before—and while it feels like many of our public safety nets are slipping away, I'm hopeful that the notion of compliance as protection for the greater good and well-being of all of us will once again be seen as an essential value in running a successful long-term business.

# THE IMPORTANCE OF
# FINDING THE RIGHT COPILOT

Helen and I had both been married twice before when we met on a biking and camping trip, each of us with separate groups on a five-day ride on the White Rim Trail in Moab, Utah. I was recently divorced, and her marriage was unraveling, and while we both left that encounter with a positive impression of each other, neither of us was in the right headspace to start a relationship. But timing is everything. Five years later we ran into each other in town in Aspen, she on crutches from a ski accident and me having just ended an ill-fated short-term relationship, and we were both in a better place. At this point, the time was right, and so was the pairing: We clicked and fit. Having a partner in a relationship who shares your values and treats you with love and kindness and compassion is the difference between pushing through turbulence and soaring in smooth air. Until then, I'm not sure I knew what the joy of flying through life truly felt like.

Princeton University psychologist Daniel Kahneman won the Nobel Prize in Economics in 2002 for his work in behavioral economics, studying how people make decisions and form judgments under conditions of uncertainty. His "prospect theory" explored the premise that we have immediate reactions to short-term gains and losses and place much more emotional weight on losses than on gains because we hate to lose. His research found that most of us aren't "foresighted utility maximizers"; we're short-term emotional reactors. I find this all

"

the time in our business, and our investment strategy takes this into account: When we first meet with clients, we do our best to assess their appetite and tolerance for risk and their overall long-term confidence in the markets. As I mentioned earlier, if we sense that they'll be easily spooked by market movement, we'll put them in a much more conservatively weighted portfolio; if they're generally optimistic about the future and have traditionally been constant investors, we'll put them in a more growth-weighted portfolio knowing they've lived through the vagaries of the market and weathered previous ups and downs emotionally and financially. Those decisions are good for us too: When the market goes down, not only do we have unhappy clients, but our own business is affected since our expenses stay the same even when our income stream falls. We're all on the same roller-coaster ride.

While we'll all do almost anything to avoid losing money, I'm most frequently asked how we protect someone's savings and how quickly we can make their savings grow. While we can and do go into detail about diversification, picking good companies with good managers through deep research, and carefully balancing our portfolio—all the ways we try to manage and balance risk—there's one threat to a person's financial security I almost never mention: divorce. Divorce almost always guarantees the eventual loss of half or more of a person's savings and net worth, yet most people don't focus on that aspect of the decision whether to remain in a marriage, which supports Kahneman's point about our failure to be "foresighted utility maximizers." If we consider another scenario with similar consequences—imagine our reaction to news that the Dow had plummeted 50 percent on any given day—it would feel like the end of the world to anyone whose financial security had disappeared overnight. When I think about quelling some client's concerns about our underperforming the S&P by a percent or two when that same client willingly gave up 50 percent of their savings to leave a marriage, it's clear that there's a blind spot in how we do this sort of calculus.

That's why I tell clients, and young people particularly, that one of the most important decisions they'll ever make in life is whom they choose as their life partner. Now, those of you who know me well might say that I'm not the most qualified person to give advice on staying married when I myself have been through two divorces, and that is absolutely true. Each failed relationship has its own specific set of reasons and circumstances for why things didn't work out, and those reasons can be debated—but what usually requires no debate is how divorce causes emotional and economic disaster for one or both parties. Having gone through my own anguish during and after my divorces and having helped countless clients through similar situations, I can attest to the sad truth of that basic fact.

Choosing the right person—your life's copilot—is likely the most important decision you'll make at any age. A partner can either help you achieve emotional and financial stability and success or hinder those things. Google's list of characteristics for a good pilot and copilot includes excellent situational awareness, strong communication skills, excellent decision-making abilities, a high level of attention to detail, the ability to remain calm under pressure, strong leadership qualities, a desire to continuously learn, and a deep understanding of teamwork, all while maintaining a focus on safety. Which are all true. But missing from that list are many other aspects that come into play when we enter into a romantic relationship with another person: great chemistry and physical attraction, social status, financial assets and stability, or feeling emotionally completed by someone who seems to fill that empty hole we have not figured out how to fill ourselves. Over the years, I've seen people, myself included, make so many of the same common mistakes in perception and judgment—ignoring both red flags and basic facts of incompatibility because we want so much to find our person, to join with someone else in an intimate way, to find a long-lasting, loving relationship. Sometimes we choose to overlook obvious problems because they're difficult to discuss and hard to resolve—issues around addiction, religion, and differentials in financial assets, how and where to spend money, whether you want children and how many and why, or the needs of children from previous marriages, to name only a few—and sometimes we're simply naive enough to think that love will cure what ails us, that we'll overcome our differences once we're settled into a stable relationship. Maybe. But it doesn't usually work that way. The time to have difficult conversations is before the wedding, not after.

Helen and I are a team. We know we can count on each other, and we have lived enough apart and together to know what issues are worth working on and fighting for and which make more sense to accept or simply let go of. All the characteristics of a good pilot and copilot apply to trust in your partner just as they do to trust in the cockpit. We both feel so lucky to have found each other, and since we have, so many of the impediments and challenges of life have become adventures and fun projects to work on together. I wish the same for everyone and can't emphasize enough how the decision about whom to share your life with will be just as important to your economic circumstances as it is to your emotional health.

# WALLY'S OPTIMIST CREED

Anyone who knows me well or who works with me knows that I'm a big believer in "The Optimist Creed," which was written in 1912 by Christian D. Larson, among the pioneers of modern motivational philosophy. In one of life's greatest ironies, I learned about "The Optimist Creed" while at the funeral of my beloved friend, college classmate, and former brother-in-law Bill Patterson, who died about fifteen years ago of a brain tumor at the too-young age of forty-eight. "The Optimist Creed" was printed in his memorial book, and while I was already prone to optimism, having absorbed my father's unwavering focus on the beauty and goodness in life, seeing Larson's specific tenets articulated and printed at a moment of deep loss forever changed me. I guess you could say it crystal-lized a set of aspirational beliefs that I'd always held but had never quite put into words.

"The Optimist Creed" imprinted itself on my mind and spirit, and I don't think there's been a day since when I haven't thought of it or recited the list out loud or silently in the morning on my drive in to work. On particularly rough days, when I'm feeling that the world is getting the best of me, I'll say the creed a few times; in moments of extreme challenge, I'll focus on a single line that feels most relevant and helpful. For me, "The Optimist Creed" is powerful; it's my version of my father's saying that above any bad-weather clouds, the sun is always shining.

Here is the version of the classic meditation that I repeat to myself daily:

Promise Yourself . . .

To be so strong that nothing can disturb my peace of mind.

To talk health, happiness, and prosperity to every person I meet.

To make all my friends feel that there is something worthwhile in them.

To look at the sunny side of everything and make my optimism come true.

To think only of the best, to work only for the best, and to expect only the best.

To be just as enthusiastic about the success of others as I am about my own.

To forget the mistakes of the past and press on to the greater achievements of the future.

To wear a cheerful expression at all times and give a smile to every living creature I meet.

To give so much time to improving myself that I have no time to criticize others.

To be too large for worry, too noble for anger, too strong for fear, and too happy to permit the presence of trouble.

While I've internalized those lines to the point that I feel they're my own, I've realized that I have my own thoughts about optimism, my own set of particular and personal beliefs that define how I see the world. I share my own "Optimist Creed" with you now, in case you might find it useful or meaningful:

Promise Yourself . . .

To lead by example instead of giving advice.

To believe the best and plan for the worst.

To talk less and listen more.

To know everyone's name and be kind, patient, curious, and humble.

To provide guidance and comfort to those who need it.

To have a service heart.

To make and follow a checklist.

To always have a project to work on and a problem to solve.

To never stop reading, learning, and recommending books to friends, family, and colleagues, even if they still haven't finished (or started) most of the ones you've pushed on them.

To eat first, then talk business.

To feel deeply and truly grateful for everything you have, and for everyone you love and everyone who loves you.

To support and comfort those you care about, to be a rock for others when they need it most, and to let others be a rock for you when you need it most.

To advise young people to work hard, earn as much as they can, live relatively frugally, try to save and invest 10 to 15 percent of their earnings each year, focus on their education, live a little each day, spend money on some special things that are fun while saving for bigger-ticket items like future housing or starting a business.

To ask your children's prospective partners, "Do you ski?"

To keep your 1947 Willys Jeep or any other thing of deep sentimental value.

To tell the bad jokes, even the bad dad jokes (especially the bad dad jokes) and ignore the cringing (there will always be cringing).

To plow your own driveway.

To get in line as early as possible for seats at Warren Buffett's annual meeting even if everyone makes fun of you for your boyish enthusiasm.

To order the weirdest thing on the menu.

To embrace nicknames like Spanky as terms of endearment.

To say yes to the next big adventure, challenge, business opportunity, or relationship—despite allergies, asthma, or fear of the unknown.

To eat all the chocolate chip cookies and to always eat them before dinner.

To take a picture of every cloud, sunset, sunrise, body of water, mountaintop, landing strip, airplane hangar, and person you love.

To remember that while beginnings are great, *"Der Endspurt ist das Allerwichtigste"*—the final sprint is the most important.

# EPILOGUE

My daughter Catherine has gone to Durango for the day. She's at the Vallecito Reservoir, representing Wally's interests in the hydroelectric facility he built forty years ago. It's his passion project and in many ways the achievement he feels most emotionally connected to.

Sam Perry, whom Wally describes as a younger version of himself and who will run Ptarmigan and the hydro facility going forward, has arranged a meeting at the facility. Attendees include representatives of the electric company, who want the project to thrive so that they will have a reliable source of clean energy going forward; the board of directors of the Pine River Irrigation District, who represent the water rights of approximately fifteen hundred farmers in the region; and representatives of the Southern Ute Indian tribe, who also own rights to the water in the reservoir and have felt that their voices have not been adequately represented in the past. It is quite an assembly of true western archetypes. As anyone from the West will tell you, it's all about water. To give you an indication of how seriously people in the West take their water rights, there is a saying: "Women are for sharing, but water is for fighting."

Into this meeting walks twenty-eight-year-old Catherine, stunning and probably trembling inside, but determined. She is one of only two women invited to attend, there to help all these men figure out how to put their outrage aside and collaborate. But she has been trained by the best—by her stepdad,

Wally—and by the end of the day, guns have been holstered and handshakes prevail.

Then Catherine asks for a moment of silence and an acknowledgment from all parties that if it weren't for Wally Obermeyer's decency, respect, and ability to listen and take all parties' interests and grievances into consideration, this assembly of people and the success of this project over the past forty years would never have happened. Everyone there feels responsible for making sure this success will continue into the future, and they all need to take a moment and think about how Wally would want them to behave in order to make it work.

Wally is home with me, eager to hear what Catherine has to say but unable to participate because fifteen months ago he was struck down by glioblastoma, which as my friend Nick Paumgarten wrote to me is "the dreadful thing, the killer of sixty-year-old men." Wally has fought an epic battle with this disease. He has used all his persistence, intellect, stamina, and positivity, but it is an enemy bigger than even his willpower and his belief that goodness ultimately prevails can overcome. At this phase of the disease, he cannot speak; he can only try his damndest to communicate to us through his eyes, and when Catherine calls with good news from that meeting, he whispers thank you and weeps.

I knew that Wally's stories, some from his childhood, are legend, but when Dana and Ali proposed the idea of writing a book, I didn't realize what a good idea it would be. Not only have we relived his life and reconnected with memories long ignored, but we grew so much closer in the process. Why do some memories linger and others fade? Which experiences propel us forward, and which prevent us from fulfilling our potential? We had hours alone together to explore these ideas in depth, in hotels and Airbnbs in the various cities we moved to as we pursued every potential cure. We had the opportunity to dig into the emotions behind the stories and in many instances learn anew from them. I got to know my husband in an even more intimate and profound way, something which surprised me because I thought I knew him so well before. Wally puts the most positive spin on everything. He is quiet; he doesn't like to be the center of attention. But as I dug deeper into many of his early memories, I began to understand the pain behind some of those self-defensive attributes.

Over the years we were married, I would often be asked to go on girls' trips or to do things that didn't include Wally. I said no to most of them, partially because after so many years without a true partner, someone I could totally and completely rely on and be myself with, I never wanted to leave him. I always wanted more of his time. But there was something else. I told my best friends that I had to be careful with him; he was sensitive in a way I had not experienced before, there was a fragility in him that I was determined to fix. I needed to have him know he could rely completely on me and that I was not going to hurt him. It was important to me to have him know I was a source of security, the place where he could finally unburden himself and relax. That is how we have proceeded these past fifteen months. It sounds cliché, and those who know me know I am not a martyr (I do what I want when I want), but I told him I was going to be by his side wherever this journey was going to lead us. This past year he gave me the gift of being able to show him how much I love him. He had always done so for me in so many ways, from bringing me the foamiest latte in bed every morning to always leaving love notes in my bags and various hiding places to loving my daughters and my parents as his own. But at the end, it was the two of us traveling the world looking for a cure. We walked this final phase of his life hand in hand, as my friend Eric pointed out, one heart, one mind, one soul. I feel I am the luckiest woman alive to have spent the past fifteen years as Wally Obermeyer's wife, lover, soulmate.

I have no answers for why someone so good gets struck down just at the moment they are about to start unwinding and letting others take on the burdens they have shouldered for so long. But I tell my daughters and friends, who are as devastated as I am, that the best way to honor Wally is to live his attributes: Be a romantic, be humble, work hard, be thrifty, love deeply and uncompromisingly, be nerdy, love the outdoors, be amazed by the beauty of our surroundings, be grateful for all of it.

In the last days, when Wally was still able to talk, the only times he truly broke down were when he said how much he was going to miss people.

Not to laugh with Steve, or be astounded by Fred's logic—his "Fredisms," as Wally called them—not to fly with Andrew or Micah, laugh at Ernie's jokes, share the deepest feelings and more travels with Allen, be inspired by Rick's compassion and commitment to community, share his passion for fishing and finance with Gilchrist and Harry, learn more about sports and seek more advice from Todd, share the fondest memories from college with Jamie and Fereed, love the quiet moments of wisdom and guitar with Adam, build paradise with Claudious, learn more about history and friendship from David, be curious with Gary, always learn some new fact from John, share some wisdom and appreciate new insights from everyone at OWP, be deeply inspired by Eric's quest for knowledge and all he managed to achieve, climb more mountains, track more elk, share a multitude of memories, and his complete respect and love for Tom.

He simply couldn't bear the pain of thinking about not seeing more of Klaus, Nome, Henry, Suzan, Klausie, Michael, Jenny, Cilly, Klaus, and Ute.

These moments of despair were tough to witness, but none were like the utter defeat he exuded when thinking about not seeing his wonderful grandchildren grow up; not being able to see his stepdaughters' achievements and hopefully see them marry, have their own families, and feel the love he knows is possible; not having more and more and more time with all of his children and their partners—these were the unbearable moments when I left the room, because I could not watch.

We all carry you in our hearts, Wally, and you will continue to inspire us every day from now until forever. You are truly my soulmate, and I know our journey is not over.

*—Helen Obermeyer, May 2025*
*Aspen, Colorado*

ACKNOWLEDGMENTS AND
AUTHOR'S NOTE

In April 2024, Wally and I were living in Durham, North Carolina, where Wally was being treated for glioblastoma at the Preston Robert Tisch Brain Tumor Center. We had safely landed there with the help of our dear friends Laurie and Patsy Tisch in the care of Dr. Henry Friedman, who is recognized as an innovative leader in the treatment of this disease. Wally had just been diagnosed a month before and had already gone through surgery, and we were realizing that we would likely be in Durham for many months. Dana and Ali suggested that Wally write a book while he was recovering—a founder's manual, if you will. They wanted something they could give to new employees and new and existing clients to help them understand Wally's business philosophy and the principles upon which he built the firm into the success it is today.

When it became clear that as talented as he was in many areas, narrative writing was not going to be one of Wally's fortes, I suggested that I interview him, create a story people might enjoy, read it to him, and we could proceed like that and see where it took us. Knowing so many of the early stories of his life, I knew you couldn't talk about Wally's current success without going back to his childhood to understand where his philosophy of life emanated from. So we started there. I remember reading aloud to him an early draft of chapter one. He listened and was quiet. When I asked him if the facts as he knew them were correct, he said yes and paused. Then there was a longer pause. When I asked him if it sounded right, he paused again. Then he flashed that beautiful smile and said, "I love it! I want to know that guy!" And so we proceeded. It was a joy right down to the end.

I quickly realized, however, that I really didn't know anything about writing a book. I reached out to Adrienne Brodeur, a great friend, accomplished author, and the executive director of Aspen Words, of which Wally and I were supporters. She introduced us to Laura Zigman, who has published six novels to date and ghostwritten or collaborated on many more. The connection with both me and Wally was instantaneous. With Laura by our side every step of the way, we were off and running. It was only later that we found out she had lost her dad to glioblastoma, so not only would she be our literary guide, she would become our spiritual guide too. She and Catherine interviewed team members and clients for the business portion, and once the manuscript was finished, Laura Obermeyer spent hours gathering and scanning all the photos. Celia Johnson, Maria Gagliano, Karl Spurzem, Dan Avant Blachman, and Beth Blachman at The Pub Pros Inc. edited, designed, and produced this book quickly and beautifully. It has been a great collaboration.

Wally is not here today to write these acknowledgments, but I know most of the people he would want me to mention. If I have forgotten someone, I deeply apologize.

Thank you to the crew team and the pals from Harvard who jumped in with anecdotes and wonderful memories and who didn't hesitate for a second to pull an oar and help out in any way possible when they heard of Wally's diagnosis: Jamie O'Donnell, John Stevenson, Bard Cosman, Albert Leger, Bruce Beall, Mike Aronow, Pat Bennett, Phil Talbert, Justin Kermond, Edd Fleming, Bill Patterson, and the coxswain, Mike Phillips. Other college supporters include Keith Rogal, Bruce Holley, Bill Cross, and Fereed Mangalji.

Many thanks to the team from Sport Obermeyer and all those dedicated to the continuation of Ptarmigan and the Vallecito hydroelectric project: Mark Whalen, Katy Wabiszewski, Tim Belinski, Brett Anderson, Joe Brown, Christy Duran, Michael Canterbury, Monty Deckerd, John Estes, Barry Post, Brent Gardner, Ken Beck, and, most of all, Eric Jacobson, Robert Lee, Kourtney Hadrick, and the best possible steward to continue what Wally started, Samuel Perry.

A world of respect for Janice (Jan) Hammond, Marshall Fisher, and Ananth Raman. Such fun working on that HBS case study together.

To the team at Obermeyer Wealth Partners, who are mentioned throughout the book but whom I'll never be able to thank enough: Ali Phillips, Dana Nightingale, Charlton Rugg, Roger Hennefeld, Adam Savin, Nick Barnes, Bret Hirsh, Brian Brady, Brooke Gais, Patrick Yarborough, Kimbo Brown-Shirato, Hayden Porter, Anna Buckley, Elise Wood, Sean McGechie, Naomi Seldin, Jody Dible, Molly Hartzler, Mikaela Durben, and the ever-loyal Christine Goodendorf. Others indispensable to the success of the firm were Mary Ryerson and Janet Roberts.

The Gates Family Foundation opened our world to the need in Colorado. Under your incredible leadership, Tom Gougeon, you have made Colorado a more compassionate place in so many ways along with your excellent team: Ana Soler, Amanda Hill, Whitney Johnson, Carol Menard, Lisa Rucher, Anna Schmid. For the opportunity to have experienced all of this, my undying gratitude to Diane Gates and Wes Brown.

Christy Mahon, Chris Lane, and so many wonderful board members at ACES: Amy Margerum, Sam Brown, Daniel Shaw. The great team at Denver Museum of Nature and Science under George Sparks. Martha Cochran at Aspen Valley Land Trust. Annie Oppenheim and Nick Favaloro at $(HS)^2$ and the Squared Network. Wally learned so much from all of you.

With gratitude to Wally's incredible medical teams: first and foremost, Dr. Ronald Colson at CU Anschutz, who was always there for us. Thank you! The incredibly caring team at Aspen Valley Hospital: Nancee Dodge, Maria Dungo, Hogan, Jenna, Nicole, Lexi Bradfield, Jeannie, and Melissa. At Duke Cancer Center, Henry Friedman, Rosemary Ketring, Renee Raynor. At Dana-Farber Cancer Center: Ugonma Chukwueke and Celia Speth. The forward-thinking doctors whom we hope hold the key to future success: Pam Contag at BioEclipse, Dr. Saskia Biskup, Veit Scheble, Olga Maksimovic, and Sarap at CeGat Zentrum für Ambulante Onkologie in Tübingen, Germany. Dr. Stephen Bagley, University of Pennsylvania Medical Center, and the incredibly caring and competent hospice team: Oanh Hoang, Daisy Salinas, Shayanne Perez, Darnell Langley. Peg O'Brien, you led us through the veil with poetry and song, and you bring comfort to everyone you meet: No words are adequate.

To the friends on whose shoulders we leaned and cried—you all are the best gift anyone could ask for: Amy and Gilchrist Berg, Suzanne Bober and Steve Kahn, Margot Bush, Isa Catto and Daniel Shaw, Caroline and Floyd Converse, Shanta and Claudious Culmer, Austin Corona, Leslie DeRosa, John and Lauren Driscoll, Sue and Tom Durkin, Jenny and Tom Eddy, Jaimie and David Field, Jane and Allen Grossman, Teresa Hall, Bentley and Doug Rager, Becky Henry and Harry Gruner, Barbara (BV) and Telly Hoimes, Liz and Keith Howie, Julie and Michael

Kennedy, Melony and Adam Lewis, Wendy and Todd Mitchell, Michael and Jenny Obermeyer, Jamie and Sarah O'Donnell, Kristi and Tim Patterson, Catherine and Tom Reagan, Lisanne and Jim Rogers, Martine and Jeffrey Russell, Claire and Martin Solomon, Zibby and Rick Schwartz, Electra Toub and Peter Soros, Nancy and Tom Wall, and so many others too numerous to mention.

Those who share the love of flight: Craig Angus, Jeff Yusem, Andrew Doremus, Peter Hudder, Bubba Collins, Micah Harrison, Kevin Fenske, Shane Alexander, Bruce Gordon, and Jane Pargiter.

Our families, who are forever with us and never fail us: Klaus, Nome, Henry, Catherine, Suzan, Klaus Jr., Laura, Erik, Karl, Michael, Jenny, Cilly, Klaus, Ute, and all the Obermeyers. Carol and Jim Swiggett, Clif, Nelda, Dylan, and Jack Swiggett. Hank, Lisa, Jamie, and Blake Swiggett and Bailey, Andrew, and Henry Preusse.

Natalie, Matt, William, Emma, and Eleanor Hunter, whose antics and growth kept us moving forward in love through constant care and beautiful photographs. Kyra and Catherine Ward, who didn't hesitate, dropped everything, came, and did not ever shy away. You sustained Wally with your deep love. We were and will continue to be family in the very best sense of the word. What a joy it has been, what a legacy we all will continue to live up to.

Wally, this book is 100 percent an acknowledgment of you and the impact you have had on so many. You showed more courage and lived more life in your way too brief sixty-eight years. Every person on this page and so many, many, many more owe some of the best that we are to the moments we spent with you.

Rest in peace.

Wally founded Obermeyer Asset Management, now Obermeyer Wealth Partners, after serving as regional vice president of Heritage Trust and Asset Management from 1994 to 1997. He had a broad range of business and financial experience, including managing his family's ski apparel business and founding a hydroelectric power generation company. Wally earned his MBA from Harvard Business School and a BA, cum laude, from Harvard College. Wally chaired the board of the Denver Museum of Nature & Science Foundation and was on the boards of the Aspen Center for Environmental Studies and the Aspen Valley Land Trust. He was an underwriter of Aspen Words and (HS)2 and the Squared Network and a contributor at the Aspen Institute and the Aspen Music Festival. He was most appreciative and proud of his twelve-year term on the board of the Gates Family Foundation, where he also chaired the Investment Advisory Committee.

Wally was recognized for more than a decade in leading industry rankings, most recently by Forbes ("Top Wealth Advisors" in 2025 and "Best-in-State Wealth Advisors" in 2025) and Barron's ("Top 100 Independent Advisors" in 2024 and "America's Top Independent Advisors" in 2025). He was also one of Barron's 2019 Hall of Fame advisors in recognition of being ranked on the Top 100 list for over ten years. A visionary, Wally built his firm on the foundation of trust, integrity, and unwavering dedication to clients.

Last trip, fulfilling a lifelong desire to see the Panama Canal

Joy of being a grandfather

From "The Optimist Creed": Give every living creature a smile.

Celebrating Mother Ganges on a trip with Tom and Kristi

Oktoberfest at Hoffbrau Haus

African adventures

Happiness, my guitar in my library on Windermere Island

Always seeking more wisdom

Bliss, picnic in the Alps after a long hike

More wonderful travel adventures

Happy in the Bahamas: Catherine, Kyra, me, Helen, and Austin

Family ski day on the trail named for my dad

My signature happy face

Celebrating at Bemelmans Bar, NYC

Learning to love sailing

Loving being a dad

Reading time with Natalie

Loving Kyra

Taking our band on the road, Kyra and me

Happy Bahamas afternoons

Celebrating college graduation

Proud stepdad, law school graduation

Loving Catherine

Sailing adventure

Thoughtful moments

African afternoons

Always laughing

Cuban nights

Cuban days

Proud stepdad, COVID-style college graduation

So many summits

A surprise proposal

Blissful years

Happy in Rajasthan

Kilimanjaro

Bryce Canyon

Grand Canyon, bike trip

Visiting Eric's office in DC

Mount Harvard summit

Caught! Photo booth at our wedding

Rwanda trekking

Placing a Diya prayer in the Ganges at Varanasi

Best of friends in the Bahamas

Best of friends in Aspen

Susan and Fred for my 60th in Napa

Steve and Tom after fishing Taylor River

My great pal Telly

Eric at the National Cathedral, DC

Gilchrist and Fred, best of friends